Hip Santa Cruz 5

*First-person Accounts of
the Hip Culture of Santa Cruz
in the 1960s, 1970s, and 1980s*

2nd Edition, Revised and Extended

*Edited by T.Mike Walker
with the assistance of Ralph H. Abraham*

*Epigraph Books
Rhinebeck, New York*

Hip Santa Cruz 5. First-person accounts of the Hip Culture of Santa Cruz, California in the 1960s, 1970s, and 1980s.

Copyright 2020 by Ralph H. Abraham. All rights reserved.

No part of this book may be used or reproduced in any manner without written permission from the publisher except in critical articles and reviews.

For information contact:
Epigraph Publishing Service
22 East Market Street, Suite 304
Rhinebeck, New York 12572
www.epigraphPS.com

Book Design by Deb Shayne

ISBN 978-1-951937-14-0
Library of Congress Control Number: 2020902041

Bulk purchase discounts for educational or promotional purposes are available. Contact the publisher for more information.

CONTENTS

Preface	*6*
Ch. 1. Marcellus Barns by T. Mike Walker	7
Ch. 2. Until We're Free by Ann J. Simonton	14
Ch. 3. Joe Schultz by T. Mike Walker	24
Ch. 4. Manny Santana by Don Monkerud	29
Ch. 5. Chez Ray and Sleazy D by Dean Quarnstorm	40
Ch. 6. William James Association Prison Art Project by Jack Bowers	55
Ch. 7. Jerry Kamstra and the Creative Lineage by Daniel Yaryan	68
Ch. 8. Memories by Daniel Wenger	75
Ch. 9. Tom Noddy, the Bubble Man by Tom Noddy	86
Ch. 10. I Can Do This Work! by Karen Ehrlich	93
Ch. 11. My Hip Santa Cruz History by Dan Phillips	106
Ch. 12. Hip Pocket Bookstore Obscenity Case by Stanley D. Stevens	113
Ch. 13. Melyssa Demma by Ralph Abraham	134
Ch. 14. Photo Gallery by Andrew Bailey	141

Ch. 15. One Night at the Barn
        by Louie Bacigalupi   164
Ch. 16. Beard House, UCSC, 1967
        by Douglas Col   167

INDEX   171

Ralph and T. Mike, 1971

Preface
by T. Mike Walker

Even as we finished Volume 4 of Hip Santa Cruz, we knew we needed at least one more book to include a minimum of stories needed to establish the birth and rapid growth of a world-wide revolutionary progressive counter-culture. We are convinced that Spiritual awakenings triggered by wide use of Psychedelics contributed greatly to our personal and cultural transformations

Over the past 60 years we have created cultural, legal and political changes which have profoundly transformed millions of lives for the better.

The stories you are about to read reflect the experiences of artists, scientists, musicians, teachers, writers, and ordinary people responding and adapting to extraordinary times. Santa Cruz was one of the crucial incubators of the Aquarian Age. Caught between the University of California at Santa Cruz on one side and Cabrillo Community College on the other, this quiet retirement community was catapulted into the 20th century by an sudden influx of new ideas and a demand for new ways to live, think, and breathe.

Chapter 1: Marcellus Barns
by T. Mike Walker

I was raised back on the east coast in New York City. Back in 1960 we had a cultural shock wave which began in Greenwich Village and called up a whole bunch of us, starting with my best friend Dino Valenti and his band, bringing out Bob Dylan, Noel Stuke of Peter, Paul and Mary, Leonard Cohen, Lou Gossett Jr., Joan Baez, Fred Neal, Karen Dalton, just to name a few. That was before they started getting political, but their songs were being recognized as stories about our times and how people were feeling. The music was being widely dispersed and all over the country people were listening and many of us started acting on our beliefs, including me. It was time for everyone to stand up for what we believed and wanted to stand up for! We were gifted, we were the children of freedom and war and everything else that goes along with it. And so we were saying things, using our voices in every way.

Those were formative times in our nation and my friend Richie Havens wrote all about that summer in his book *They Can't Hide Us Anymore*: "I remember a fellow who was simply called Marcellus, the first man I ever saw with dreadlocks, the hair style later popularized by the Rastafarian. Marcellus also was an African American who stepped up on folk stages and knocked people out with classical pieces for the Spanish guitar. Marcellus and Dino Valenti were best friends. They never went anywhere without each other. They had deep love and mutual resect for each other, the rarest display of true brotherhood I'd ever seen...Marcellus and Dino would become my guides to the future in many ways."*

Marcellus was born in 1940, and was 27 when he arrived in California. "I moved to Santa Cruz in September of 1967, right after the Monterey Pop Festival. This was at a time when communes were just coming into play, people gathering in groups collectively, some close, others far away, trying to find a common ground to live together. So that was my introduction to Life here in Santa Cruz. Communal living wasn't happening anywhere else that I knew of, certainly not in New York. The first commune I encountered was Holiday Lodge in Ben Lomond. There are many pictures of me then in the publication by Holly (*Inside A Hippy Commune* by Holly Harmon).

"I arrived there with a drum slung on my back, sat down on a tree stump and started playing. The party got longer and I kept on playing until one day went by and two days went by and I'm still playing, and by the third day it started to calm down. People were tired, but everything seemed to meld, and they said to me: Well, you're one of us now! You don't have anywhere else to go, so you're stuck here with us.

"And I said, Cool! I found a home, at least for a few months.

"Those were the juicy times, with everyone playing music, having fun, tripping out, meeting new folks: the old ones, the young ones, the baby ones, the naked ones, people of all sizes, colors, languages, it didn't matter, we were all together. We cooked together, ate together, slept together, and took care of one another as we learned to forage and garden and share the spiritual aspects of our lives. Because it was a learning experience, everybody was learning at a rapid rate, and the community itself was somewhat taken aback from what was happening, but everybody kept going forward. That to me was the essence of growth and I was happy just to be involved. Then I discovered there was also an inner-commune connection, so I decided to check out another commune.

"After Ben Lomond I moved to The Family on Trout Gulch Road in Aptos. I literally got scooped up from one commune scene to the next. When I arrived, Joe Lysowski was painting Ken Kesey's Prankster Bus at The Family commune. There was a big house, a barn with stalls for a couple of horses, and lots of Kesey's friends & relatives from La Honda who would stop at The Family on their way back and forth from Oregon to LA. That was in '67.

"Along with all the people at the commune, there was this one young really big puppy named Sherman, who sat on the floor looking right into me and said, 'Hello!' inside my head. This was the first Great Dane I ever met and I was impressed. He belonged to Bob, the guy who was running the commune. I forget his last name. He was from Kentucky, a really far-out guy, a good leader, a real cool dude with sparkly blue eyes and blue robes and a good smile. Lots of folks were wearing robes and other fancy fineries back then, holding fairy-tale weddings and shit like that. Sherman was Bob's dog, but no one knew how he arrived at the commune. They used to hold acid parties, and I realized when we met that the dog had already been tripping. After a few months I got hold of a bicycle and decided to explore the neighborhood, so I would wake up early in the morning and ride down to the beach. And every time I would head off on my bike, Sherman would be running right next to me. After a while, we were imprinted. I was like a young lion myself, and here was this intelligent young animal who could dig on people-things and said to me, 'Okay, I've got this people stuff figured out, do you want to learn a few dog things?'

"Anyway, it got to be noticeable that Sherman and I were teaming up, so Bob and I had a little conversation. He said, 'Hey man, that's my dog!' I agreed with him and said I didn't want any confrontations. The dog just liked to follow me to the beach and since I was new to the neighborhood, it felt good to have him with me when I rode. So we hung with that discussion for maybe a week when Bob came back and said to me, 'Look, this whole thing about who belongs to who or what? I've got to let that go because you two seem to have a bond. I dig it. I've got my own thing going too, so if that's where this is at, that's where it's at. If Sherman wants to hang with you and you're okay with it, then we can be cool with that, right?'

"Of course I agreed, and after that Sherman ran with me everywhere for the next ten years."

Marcellus was also a connecting link of consciousness, bearing psychedelic messages between communities throughout the Monterey and San Francisco Bay areas. Richie Havens sums up Marcellus's influence on many of us then: "Two of my best Village friends, Marcellus and Dino Valenti, were the first people I knew who were into LSD. Both seemed aware of its potency, both used it sparingly, mostly in each other's presence, for self-exploration and deep personal discovery. 'This is powerful stuff,' they often said. 'But you can learn a lot about yourself and you can see things in the natural world that you miss every day.'

"Dino and Marcellus reported seeing trees expand and contract as if they were breathing and they watched blades of grass grow, millimeter by millimeter. Beyond the intensity of their LSD experiences, I learned a lot about the drug by trying it twice and watching and talking to dozens upon dozens of people who were into it. Passive LSD users regularly experienced wild hallucinations that stretched the boundaries of reality beyond recognition. Aggressive or creatively curious people, like Marcellus and Dino, usually remained grounded in reality and found their senses intensified without hallucinations. While persons who hallucinated regularly conjured up things that were physically impossible, people like Marcellus and Dino never saw anything like a tree or a car flying over their next-door neighbor's house. People who came to the drug seeking an introspective adventure, or a spiritual experiment into the unknown, usually saw new aspects of the real world. Perhaps even the hairs on the back of their hands as if they were looking through microscopic eyes."**

    Marcellus continued: "I was just learning how to connect with things; I was hungry for relations. I started playing drums for Roberta Bristol's dance classes over at Cabrillo, where I met you, T. Mike. I also started playing congos with your neighbor Don McCaslin when we started jamming and put together our first band. There was also Max Hartstein's 21st Century Ensemble and all kinds of spontaneous musical awakenings, like those full-moon festivals we held on mountain tops all over the county! Everything was emerging at once, home births and organic foods, yoga meditation and psychedelic awakenings, all kinds of things started right here in these neighborhoods, and are still going on.
    One of them was the Renaissance Faire, which became a vehicle of consciousness; the Renaissance Faires spread all over the nation in every community you can imagine. Another was the Dicken's Faire in San Francisco. Of course, Ron & Phyllis Patterson who created all that are now up in the Great 'Sky Faire Above'. Above, where so many of the Faire creators have gone to when they pass out of this fantasy world into the next one. But the counter-cultures the Faire's created are still happening today, including the food, the art, the music, and yes, even the Belly Dancers who are everywhere now, along with musicians to play middle eastern music for them. Folk Music has spread! Tribal Music has spread! Even our butts have spread a little! Everything has grown up to such a magnitude now.
    "I stayed in Santa Cruz for five years, from '67 to '72, before

I moved up North and started traveling with the Faire. It seemed like a lot longer than that, but those were formative years. In '68 Nancy and I were living at your farm on Trout Gulch Road, just up from where The Family commune had been. Nancy was pregnant with our daughter Zumara, who was due to be born in July 1969 in that little house you let us stay in behind your place. Then the midwives came, Fred & Roberta were there, and Zumi's birth was quite an occasion!

"Not long after, I remember another unforgettable event when my band, The Festival of Light, was playing a gig at the Chateau Liberte' up on the old Stagecoach road near the summit. Nobody else would take the gig because it was a wake for a Biker, one of the Hells Angels. Don McCaslin was there and you were part of the band, too! The energy was so wild, that night I had to keep yelling to everyone, 'Keep playing, no brakes, keep the energy high', because the crowd was drunk and rowdy and pissed because we were a jazz boogie band and not the Grateful Dead who they expected! Finally around midnight we had to stop for a minute and we went outside where I broke out my pipe — you remember 'Big Moe?' (An 18 inch Leather wrapped and beaded, feather draped, horn-carved Sacred Pot Peace Pipe which had become a prominent feature of many a moon festival and party that summer).

"A lot of bikers came out of the bar to join us in the Brotherhood of the Pipe, and we convinced them that we were every bit as outlaw in our own weird ways as they were in theirs. When we finished smoking they were so fucked up they could hardly stand. When we went back in to play, they were in a better mood — even when that guy named Trouble threw a bench at some hecklers, we kept playing until they were too tired to fight or even dance anymore, so that by two in the morning they were hopping on their hogs and winding up the hill so we could finally pack up our instruments and go home. That was the most insane gig I even went to, and we got paid, too!

"Not long after that, the Renaissance Faire hired me full time as a Horse Guard. When I lived at The Family I used to saddle up one of the horses with Bob and one or two others and we would ride the Aptos Hills, exploring Nicene Marks State Park, so I got familiar with horses. Sherman helped me tune in to them. When the job was offered I grabbed it, and I've been working with the Faire since then. Which goes to show that every pattern of time is a little bit different, but the effects of what we did back then are still being felt today."

*From: "*they can't hide us anymore*" by Richie Havens, Avon books, 1999; pg. 41.
**they can't hide us anymore*; pgs. 267-268.

Chapter 2: Theatre Until We're Free
Ann J. Simonton

The earliest roots of theatre can be traced back to the streets, where people took part in religious and sometimes political protests. The heart of theatre's expression was to remind the controlling forces to be responsive and sensitive toward the citizenry. The interweaving of street life and street theatre proved "All the world is a stage" and became a necessary and integral expression for the people.

Throughout the centuries, theatre has distanced itself from this original purpose. For many people, celluloid's illusive perfection has created a more intense reality than watching regular sized people perform on a stage. According to Susan Sontag's On Photography, industrialized society has turned its citizens into "image junkies". She states, "Our era prefers the image to the thing, the copy to the original, the representation to the reality and appearance to being, while being aware of doing just that." Our society's favoritism toward screened images has preempted live theatre, especially politically oriented street theatre, with television and film. This elimination has not been completely successful in our unique community of Santa Cruz. Thanks to Nikki Craft, myself and the many other participants, guerrilla or street theatre is alive and well.

As a participant and often leader, I've had the opportunity to collaborate with thousands of Santa Cruz community members to remind the world that media images of violence and hate, promote violence and hate in the real world. While many are left blubbering on the sidelines, street activists have consistently proven the importance of articulating one's convictions in the public sphere.

The first time I met Nikki we immediately shared our

violent rape experiences: both were at knifepoint when we were very young. The horror for both of us continued afterward with the police severely intimidating us. We were close confidants from the moment we met. She turned to me, her face beaming, and in her Texan drawl said, "Honey, we're fixing to do a lot of work together."

At the time she was putting the final touches on her Porn Machine, a 4 by 4-foot black cube art piece, complete with a flashing marquee announcing, "Coming Soon." On the top were iridescent letters and a huge ceramic bronze dildo that, with the help of an exerciser machine, wagged back and forth with a little American Flag attached to the top. On the side was a photo essay from Hustler entitled "Dream Lover." A woman was being severely beaten and her head was finally shoved into a toilet. On another side a money wheel spun and the fourth side held a photo of three men holding a sign that read "We Stand on Our First Amendment Rights." The men's feet firmly planted on the body of a naked woman.

Nikki handed me a stack of Hustler magazines that inspired a script I wrote for the Porn Machine's voice. A husky-voiced man (Chris Notley who started the first Actor's Theatre at 1001 Center St.) read the script, as the 'Battle Hymn of the Republic' and 'Onward Christian Soldiers' played in the background. "Our women are tormented in our Porn Machine. They are tied, they are captive, they shut up. We're just Mr. Average with an urge to attack. We stand on our right to be entertained, to see them spread their ugly pink. It's distasteful. It's women. They're ours."

On March 8, 1981 we held a press conference outside Larry Flynt's LA office to celebrate our First Amendment rights and International Women's Day. Our message was, "Hustler has been tearing up women long enough, now it's time for women to start tearing up Hustler." Three women were pinned under the newly unveiled porn machine as it played patriotic music and spouted lies about women. The street action culminated in the releasing of the women, taking an ax to the machine, and destroying piles of Hustler's for the 6 o'clock news.

Nikki named our group The Preying Mantis Women's Brigade or PMWB. We never called for censorship but we did want corporate responsibility. We were pro-sexuality and nudity. We wanted to educate the populace about the contents and ramifications of teaching young men and boys to sexualize violent pornography. Sexualizing harm to women's bodies and the devaluation of their lives, curtails our freedom and options. Degrading females is too often a normal part of a male's sex education.

Our next actions were at showings of the films Texas Chainsaw Massacre and Dressed to Kill. Sidewalk tableaux were displayed: one had a body wrapped in white sheets doused with catsup, a chainsaw by the body, and the other had a dead woman (Victoria Stone) with sign next to her that read, "Violence is not Sexy." We distributed statements as we picketed the crowd going in. During a presentation of Texas Chainsaw Massacre, which was showing at the Del Mar, fifteen to twenty of us entered the rear of the theatre with signs and leaflets, just as it showed women's bodies being shoved onto meat hooks. We climbed up on stage with our signs held high until the film was stopped. A plain-clothed police photographer popped out of the projection booth snapping photos of us. As the lights came up Jack Nelson, from Men Against Rape, read a statement he had written. By the time he finished and leaflets were offered to the hostile and surprisingly young crowd, the police had completely surrounded the theatre. We filed down the ailes and out the front door chanting, "No more violence," and through police with their billy clubs poised.

Our Miss California Pageant protests began 1980 when ribbon-wrapped meat was tossed onstage during the live telecast portion of the bathing suit competition. The same meat gifts were offered to each of the judges. Three women including Nikki were hurriedly escorted out the door. No arrests were made.

In 1981, a gaudy float carrying signs that read "No More Molds for Women." "Myth California: Never Again Uncontested" and "No More Profits Off Women's Bodies," cruised around town. The float carried Myth contestants with banners such as Miss Informed, Miss Understood and Miss Ogyny. Nikki dressed in a formal and had pink curlers dotting her hair. I wore a frilly pink satin dress and a blonde wig that literally made me dizzy. The float played tunes like "Thank Heaven for Little Girls" and "Look at That Stupid Girl." We waved to the crowds and tossing Kellogg's Cornflakes. Kellogg's was an annual sponsor of Miss America franchise until 1984 when boxes, depicting Miss America Vanessa Williams, were destroyed because Penthouse published nude images of her.

On the night of the full moon, Wednesday, June 17th 1981, fifteen vials of blood were drawn from raped women, and poured onto the wooden sign of the Civic Auditorium. This was done to remind our community that promoting women as sex objects endorses rape.

A crowd of 250 protesters gathered wearing flamboyant garb for the final Saturday evening coronation. The protest was video taped by the city police from the rooftop of the Civic. We encouraged the crowd to cross the street to where the pageant goers were stepping out of Cadillacs in their formal evening attire. We chanted loudly until the police warned us they would begin arrests.

Three of us had tickets to the real event that night and

entered the auditorium. Positioned in different parts of the auditorium, we pulled out red lipstick and drew war paint on our cheeks as the swimsuit competition began. After the show we stood by the doors facing patrons leaving the event. Angry attendees yelled and shoved us as they passed.

Nikki coincided her senior ceramic show for UCSC, entitled "Is It Art or is it Politics?" with the 1982 Myth California pageant. She created an elaborate float that carried over 100 handmade Barbie Dolls. These brightly colored, highly glazed porcelain dolls all came from the same mold, but each had unique faces, gowns, and banners like Miss Understood and Miss Represented. I spent hours helping paint each of the "girls." Community sponsors were encouraged, so an attorney sponsored Miss Demeanor and a chiropractor sponsored Miss Alignment.

The group of semi-finalist dolls rotated under a dazzling ceramic world globe. The globe held a bouquet of pale penises protruding from the top, each waving a little American flag. Stickers of Nestle's logo, another promoter of Miss America, decorated the bleeding globe.

For a week before the final coronation, Nikki and I drove the Barbie Mobile around downtown Santa Cruz. We witnessed a lot of middle-aged women flipping us the bird, and despite being rear-ended by some drunk men on the mall, we were generally a welcome sight to most Santa Cruzans. The SCPD attempted to ban the float from the streets, but our astute lawyer, Ray Gruenich, reminded them of the statute allowing protestors of the Vietnam war to use obscenities like "Fuck the Draft."

In 1982 I wore the first of three meat outfits I have worn to protest the beauty pageants. The first was a greasy gown of 30 lbs. of baloney meat designed by B. Modern. I carried the sign "Judge Meat Not Women." The evening ended when an oversized dump truck filled with men in ski masks screaming, "Death to Dykes." as they hurled water balloons at us. The police easily allowed them to come near us and waited until they had emptied their cargo on us before doing anything to stop them. According to the Sentinel, police did finally cite John Deworker, Alfred Hann, Tom Dunbar, Martin Bryant, Frank Martinez, Paul Weakland and one unnamed 16 year old boy for their assault. Nikki pressed charges against these men since damage was done to her Barbie Dolls. She stood holding the broken pieces of Miss Ogyny saying, "See what happens to pretty little things who haven't learned to take care of themselves?"

When Nikki called me for a ride from the county jail after her first arrest for taking her shirt off at the beach, I felt like a mother. I explained there were far more important issues and that if she wanted to focus on going topless on a beach she was on her own. At that time I hadn't been in on the discussions she and D. A. Clarke had been having over the far-reaching implications of pornographer's and advertiser's right to use women's nude breasts to tittilate consumers for their profit, while women have no legal right to control their own bodies. After Ms. Clarke's article on this issue appeared in Matrix (November 1981) I came to understand removing our shirts is a revolutionary step toward women possessing their own bodies.

This guerrilla street scene began outside the county courthouse, after Nikki's judge refused to rule on her right to bare her breasts. Approximately twenty five women removed their shirts and stood outside the courthouse anxiously awaiting arrests. Nikki and I dressed as the symbol of blind justice, the scales we carried read, "Blind not Just." We wanted a photo of the police handcuffing Justicia. The news media hovered. The police waited by their radios for orders to begin the arrests. Nothing happened. So we paraded from the courthouse to the police station downtown singing our theme song entitled "Song of the Chest."

Song of the Chest
Sung to Cris Williamson's "Song of the Soul"
Lyrics by Theodora Kerry

Women must dress just like ladies
Or sexual Sadies
Or pre-adolescents
Bikinis on beaches are so-so
Topless is no-no
So cover your tits & repent.

Chorus:
Oh, don't bare your chests
Why don't you stay repressed?
Father knows best till the end of time.

They say our breasts are not equal
One little peek will
Drive men crazy
Our breasts must be kept just for lovers
Or dirty book covers
It's better if men pay to see.

Chorus:
Women bare their chests
Oh how men love those breasts
Oh how they'll pay till the end of time.

Sisters our breasts must be equal

They're not unique—well
Maybe they're more fun
Meant to give food to the newborn
Not meant for men's porn
They need their day in the sun

Chorus:
So we will bare our chests
No need to be oppressed
Let breasts hang free till the end of time.

C'mon let's bare our chests
Father does not know best
Let breasts hang free till the end of time.

Women, let's bare our chests
Oh how we love our breasts
Let them hang free till the end of time.
(Repeat chorus as many times as desired!)

    Nikki had been arrested on a local county State Park beach, and we eventually learned it was legal for women to go shirtless anywhere within the city limits of Santa Cruz. This absurd contradiction left Jeff Richman of Channel 8 News shaking his head and saying, "A strange thing happened in Santa Cruz today."

    On March 8th, 1982, the official members of the "Cross Your Heart Support Network" were all arrested at Sea Cliff beach for removing their shirts. I became a codefendant in the case that had, at that time, made its way to the San Francisco District Court of Appeals.

    Guerrilla theatre helps illustrate the virtually limitless possibilities of what can be done to expose sexist culture and end it. Even the smallest group can be effective, because we can transform one another's reality through our behavior. Resisting social control through street action is a healthy response to our often, unchallenged world. It's reassuring to know the streets remain somewhat free and available to use as a stage for social change. It is equally reassuring to know there are activists who have the courage to stand up in the face of adversity. I agree with Nikki's sentiments as she explained herself once in a San Jose courtroom, her voice cracking and her face wet with tears, she said, "My intent isn't to vandalize property but to bring to public attention a connection between the objectification of women in beauty pageants, pornography, and advertising, and violence against women. I have done this kind of thing before and I will do it again, until it's safe for women to walk the streets."

Orginally published in Matrix, May 1983 (edits/additions 2020).

Chapter 3: INDIA JOZE: Take a Wok on the Wild Side
by Jozseph Schultz

Before there was an India Joze, there was a Jozseph Schultz stoking a homemade sauna for my friends. The deal was to bring any sort of exotic raw ingredients for me to cook, while together we lost all sense of what was practical or possible immersed in extremes of roaring wood-fired heat and freezing plunges in an oversized tub. This early form of "Stump the Chef" with its kohlrabi, calamari, and wild chanterelles and mysterious comestibles led to some memorable feasts, but didn't pay the bills.

A galvanizing, somewhat more business-minded break occurred when Donald Richards offered his overfilled and underutilized Solarium antique shop cum deli collective to me a couple nights a week. It was lent first to a solo Joze, and then to a growing informal collaborative of crazy artists and adventurers. It was soon named, as if through a dream-like vision, India Joze. The year was 1972, a good year to prowl the thriving flea market for mismatched dinnerware to plate mismatch cuisines: Ethiopian, Provençal, Greek, Hungarian, Burmese, Persian, Brazilian, Indian, Thai, West African. Beauty emerged from the chaos of our flea-market equipped kitchen. A random boiler-sized burner crammed into a military coffee cauldron became a wok stove, with an aquarium air-pump hose coaxing the fiery Shiva spirits around a huge Chinatown wok.

Less than a couple of years in, coke dealers with big plans bought the building and kicked all renters out of the garden refuge we created (now the Crepe Place). So the already legendary Joze's low budget, yet amazingly ambitious, Indian Thali dinners with their dozen distinct flavors and textures on one $2.75 platter, had to find a new home.

Find one we did, in 1974. Sunnyside Cafe, a former bakery-turned-greasy-spoon, next to the Brady's Yacht Club dive bar on Seabright Avenue, welcomed us into an unlikely association. Frank de Palma, AKA Greasy Frank, allowed our crew to transform his checked plastic tablecloth vibe every afternoon. Beth Regardz presided over a transformative alchemy of the traditional diner into whimsical artistic chic. Under colorful Asian umbrella sconces and Japanese paper lanterns, guests were greeted with lemon-infused steaming towels with self-laundered linens (handled by the moonlighting journalist Michael Fox, self-styled "pyro-linen-ologist") to wash away our urban grime in preparation for the sublime.

India Joze grew. Spectacular Joze Bundt cakes, carrot cakes and berry cheesecakes graced many local restaurants. Their first 5-star baker Kathy Niven, Cordon Bleu trained, brought the first fresh baked croissants to Santa Cruz, along with her chocolate éclairs, tortes, meringues, and custards. Her expertise wowed an audition with artists from the downtown Art Center in search of a suitable restaurant tenant. India Joze soon opened inside 1001 Center Street in 1977. Suddenly there were dozens of employees, and Joze's renegade leaders themselves were along for the ride. But before long the managerial and public relations skills of Jennifer Cochran, Kate Nahan, Tom Brezsny, Ann Wasserman, Tom Ellison, Joan Lintz — and others too numerous to mention — carried matters beyond all expectations. Joze exploded on the cultural scene of Santa Cruz and was soon known up and down the Cali coast as the culinary adventure destination.

However, it was the lowly and local calamari, whose time had arrived, that struck the perfect tone of artistic, gastronomic, and cultural notes all at once. In 1979 all elements came together in the first annual Calamari Festival, soon a major Santa Cruz yearly event, with thousands of eaters, artists, and fellow revelers. A full on Squid Parade, marshaled by Fast Edy in an Asian themed turquoise silk dress with a matching silk tentacle headdress who led the processional, all costumed and festooned, from the restaurant, a mile and a half down onto the Santa Cruz wharf and open sea.

There were calamari cooking classes, juried art shows, The Calamari Cookbook, The Calamari Chorus (sung to Handel's Hallelujah Chorus), Squid Calendars, clothing, postcards, lectures, Calamari Cabaret Theatre, epic Calamari Dim Sum nights with dishes, drinks and desserts of nearly 100 different squid styles. The extraordinary elegance of Beth Regardz' graphics were everywhere. We even hosted a preacher. A. West donned his signature blinding white suit, shouted a spicy Pentecoastal Squidly sermon, with a genuine southern twang, offered undying and never-ending praise for Ca-la-mar-i Sal(i)-va-tion.) The frenzy of feeding fury carried all along for the ride beyond blitz into a kind of beatific righteous collective high. Even the alley-way between the Art Center and Goodwill shared the Jozed cephalopod's glow and was ceremonially re-named 'Squid Row' with mayoral ribbon cutting and champagne toasts.

In these wild decades Santa Cruz creative intelligentsia et al, were mesmerized by Monterey Bay's own Lolligo Opalensces, celebrating this amazing, sweet, fresh local cephalopod and placing it rightfully on the North American culinary map of genius. And Joze was its willing and humbly conspiring ambassador.

Then there were the many global Food Festivals, from Brazilian Carnival, Spanish Flamenco, Now Rooz Persian New Year Feasts, to Chickpea Festivals, and Flower Festivals every May. Each immersion included sumptuous food rituals including dozens of dishes from around the world with a history of culture through cuisine. Our collective and vast stretch of the imagination allowed talents of luminaries like David Jackman (now of 'Chocolate') Jonathan Glass (now of 'Avanti'), Paul Lenik, Aimee Page (wedding cakes for the stars, and ours), Aaron Gallegos, Raj Weeresekare (now of 'Malabar' Cafe), Robert Haavie and many more to find their shine. Joze's commitment to fresh and unconventional foods led to Fungus Festivals with Joze teaming up with a growing number of local fungophiles. Then came years of collaboration with Shakespeare Santa Cruz creating Elizabethan picnics for theatregoers and much more.

Between the late night cafe hours (open til 3:00am) with legendary Joze Chai, the foods and wry humor of India Joze defined the 80s and 90s in Santa Cruz's cultural scene. Born Again Pork Benedict for Sunday brunch, a tangy cold Gin-Gin cooler, Lemon Poppy Seed cake, Persian Chicken crowned with ruby pomegranate seeds and fresh mint, Chocolate Truffles, Mousse cake and Mud Pie all led to serious edible ecstasy for Santa Cruz and beyond. Over the top visionary culinary exuberance, with a side of humor, characterized our renegade collective, with forays to San Francisco in search of chicken wattles to complete a celebration of the sophisticated cuisine of the court of Louis XIV, to a Russian Easter Feast replete with a cold salmon mousse, saffron pâté, blini.....

India Joze was profiled in the New York Times (1990) and The Washington Post (1996). My recipe for Joze Hashbrowns was even reviewed by the Boston Globe. I was flown to speak at the Smithsonian (1994).

Then there were formal graduations of 1200 students & families, weddings, reunions, first dates, foodies, students, professors: everyone found a culinary niche somewhere inside the India Joze arena. It was food, affordable enough for everyone, and good enough for anyone. What was not to like? All fresh and made from scratch remains a rare experience very few restaurants can ever achieve.

We were all in love with the world of food, all of it. From the sublime to the sordid, Joze embraced the full spectrum of human expression.

Today, as the era of big restaurants and large community gatherings seems impossibly distant, the ecstatic memories and traditions of India Joze remind us all that great things may yet be possible.

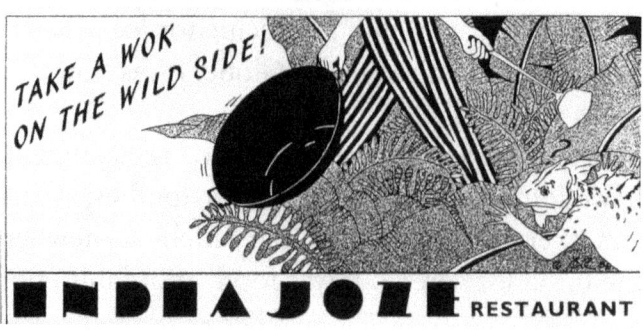

Chapter 4: A Kid from Watts Moves North:
Manny Santana
Interview by Don Monkerud

Sixty years ago, Santa Cruz County was a rural, agricultural and retirement community. With the building of Cabrillo College and UCSC, which attracted creative, freethinking people, the nature of the community began to change. Manny Santana came as a young artist and stayed to play an important role in developing housing, business cooperative ventures and culture for a growing Latino population. He also played a key role in supporting progressive political candidates in Santa Cruz County.

Manny established the well-known Manuel's Mexican Restaurant in Aptos; supported Cesar Chavez, the grape workers strike, and Chicano civil rights; lead CCCDC (Central Coast Counties Development Corp.) to promote rural economic development; and founded a farmer's co-op at the San Jerardo labor camp in Monterey County. He also served on the U.C. Water Resources Advisory Board, as a Fellow at UCSC Merrill College, on the Board of Directors of the Bear Republic Theater Company, and as president of the Cabrillo Music Festival in the 1970s and 80s.

A man with creative intelligence and boundless curiosity and energy, he raised a family, started additional restaurants in San Juan Bautista and Watsonville, designed his own house, and spent over 20 years painting and developing his artistic visions. If there are still Renaissance type activists and thinkers, Manny certainty qualified.

My first encounter with Manny Santana was in the early 1970s when I went to his restaurant to eat traditional enchiladas and tamales and listen to Steve Peterson play flamenco music. We crossed paths when I reported on the

San Jerardo labor camp housing project in 1976, a project that housed 60 farmworkers and their families near King City. I knew of his support for the creation of Cabrillo College and his role as a progressive voice in the local Democratic Party. Years later, after I moved away to work in Silicon Valley and after I returned, I visited him in his painting studio on the Westside in Santa Cruz. When I mentioned a project to explore the origins of creativity in Santa Cruz, Manny was an open and enthusiastic participant. The interview proceeded amid racks of his lush, color paintings, and swirls of fog outside.

In some ways, Manny's story includes the starving artists cliché in cultures around the world, where making a living forces many to abandon their art. The realities of supporting a family forces many young artists to get a job, and Manny was no exception.

In 1961 he wondered what he would do after studying art and painting for several years — the world wasn't beating a path to his door or buying his paintings, and he had two children and a wife to support. How to make a living? Al Johnsen, a ceramist friend and mentor from the Los Angeles County Art Institute who had moved to Santa Cruz two years earlier, called Manny with a job offer at just the right time. Would Manny move to Santa Cruz and help him paint houses? Manny took him up on the offer. Back then it wasn't easy to make a living in the area, and Manny started working for $1 an hour. His wife, who left her job at the L.A. County Board of Education Personnel Department, landed a job as a secretary for the Pajaro Valley School District.

Except for the invisible color line that Manny encountered in Watsonville — Mexicans on one side, whites on the other — he was happy with the fledgling artistic and creative life he found in Santa Cruz. Then he discovered the Sticky Wicket in Aptos, a gathering place for people like Ken Kesey, a beginning novelist; Lou Harrison, a composer who waited tables and washed dishes; and Ted Taves, a music teacher at Cabrillo who helped start the Cabrillo Music Festival. These and others displayed their art on the walls or spontaneously got up to read poetry, play the guitar or start a debate. They set up a stage next door in a vacant field and held chamber music recitals until the county shut them down for not having a permit.

"There were lots of unusual people involved in the arts back then," recalled Manny. "There were people from San Francisco: artists, young musicians, composers, poets and writers just hanging out. It was exciting and stimulating, just right for me because I was still growing up. These were interesting times in a conservative retirement community. It was one goddamn concentration of manic brainpower."

His time at the Sticky Wicket also provided Manny with contacts for additional jobs. Lou Harrison had a house to paint, as did Roy Rydell and others. Although economic survival remained difficult, Manny hung on, painting houses and forming relationships with a network in the artistic and progressive community that would last a lifetime. When I interviewed Manny, he commented that he had come a long way from his Los Angeles roots.

At the start of the 20th century, his mother's older sister brought Manny's mother across the border from Chihuahua, Mexico to Chino, California in a covered wagon. Born in 1927 in Los Angeles, Manny grew up in Watts and Compton. His father left the family and returned to Mexico where he built machinery, had another 16 children, and died at age 98. Manny's mother married a barber and Manny grew up in what he describes as "a wonderful and unusual mix of human beings", going back and forth between Mexico and the U.S.

In the 1930s and 40s, Watts consisted of rural communities, some without electricity, but surrounded by open space where his uncle raised sheep and goats and dug wells for homesteads. Manny didn't do well in school unless he enjoyed the subject. When he was 17 — shortly after WWII started — he attended Jordan High School and became involved in social issues and teen centers. Seeking support for the centers in wider Los Angeles, he spoke to city councils, church groups and other organizations. The process led him to understand the disparity between social classes and set the basis for his involvement in Democratic politics.

During his high school years, the Zoot Suit riots brought sailors into the Latino community where they beat up young men who wore oversized jackets with padded shoulders and baggy, tight-cuffed, high-waisted pants, sometimes accented with long watch chains and suspenders. Although a loner, Manny joined his friends as they lined up beside the Red Line tracks, the L.A. electric rail cars that ran from L.A. to Long Beach and gave servicemen free rides. They threw rocks to chase the sailors out of the neighborhood. During this time, he met his first community organizer and became active in politics. He learned that if people in the community wanted healthcare, hospitals and parks, they would have to organize and lobby the government.

Manny took Latin, loved listening to music and, in school, read everything he could get his hands on. His teachers nurtured his healthy curiosity, although Manny didn't know how to express his enthusiasm after the ideas fired his imagination. To get him out of the academic classes, the school placed him in a journalism class where he discovered writing. He improved his writing skills, became the editor of the high school paper, and raised money to increase the paper's circulation.

Immediately upon graduation from high school in 1944, Manny was drafted into the army. There he met college-educated men and became aware of his own lack of education. During basic infantry training at Camp Roberts in California, Manny was injured and hospitalized. Upon his recovery, the war ended and he was discharged. Returning to Watts, he bummed around at various jobs, unloading freight cars by hand and working in a lighting factory, an electrical plant and a foundry. The GI Bill offered open admission to veterans at East L.A. Junior College and Manny thought, "What the hell, why not try school?" He soon discovered that his functional use of grammar was much better than his academic knowledge, and he had lots to learn.

"These were the best years of my life," Manny recalled. "Everybody was a veteran, including all the teachers, and there was an equality in class that was exciting. Many veterans had been exposed to political history, and socialism and communism weren't such bad things then. Classes offered high-quality debates between the class and the professor, and the debates would continue during lunchtime in the cafeteria. This was the first time I got a larger intellectual view of things. It lasted about two years and then the McCarthy period snapped in. People couldn't believe how rapidly and completely it all ended."

One manifestation of McCarthy inspired anti-Communist repression was the clearance of any speakers on campus with the college administration. Although approval hadn't been required previously, the administration began to cancel speakers that students brought to campus. The FBI questioned students about the political views of their teachers. When Manny transferred to L.A. State College, one professor stated that he didn't want any pinkos, commies, or socialists in his class. Manny asked who would judge their politics and the

Don Monkerud   33

professor responded, "Don't worry kid, I'll decide." Manny had been involved in the political process long enough to recognize a serious problem. The attitudes of the teachers at L.A. State appalled him. For example, one instructor told Manny that more Mexicans were being allowed through the educational system and, if he was lucky, he could get a teaching job.

"It was a real eye opener," Manny said. "It wasn't what I needed. I'd seen lots of discrimination and when I got to college I didn't expect to see this kind of stupidity. These instructors had graduate degrees and were social idiots. It was kind of discouraging."

Manny walked precincts for the Democratic Party, going door-to-door to get out the vote. He joined the first chapter of the ACLU in Orange County to protect an African American family that moved into the area. They were being harassed by members of the community who poured concrete down their toilet. He worked to increase the number of minorities living in housing projects and to increase membership in the ACLU. These and similar projects would engage him throughout his life.

"I've always been involved in causes, I can't seem to get away from them," Manny explained. "The issues are commonplace and that's the hell of it: the loyalty oath, housing, jobs, privacy from government, prejudice in hiring. The things we were fighting in Watts after the Zoot Suit riots are worse now than they were then. Though some of the work done during that time is beginning to pay off, some things have gotten worse. It's still here."

While in college, Manny observed classes in East Los Angles Elementary schools where he found some of the worst teachers he'd ever seen. Although he was training to become a teacher, he realized that he'd be kicked out for his views.

There was no way he could teach in such schools, and keep his mouth shut about the poor quality of education he found there. Manny decided to quit school and take a vacation. When he went to his abnormal psychology instructor to drop the class, she told him that she'd taken the doodles he drew during class and thrown in the wastebasket and showed them to an instructor in the art department. The teacher said Manny showed talent and suggested that he switch his major to art. With her advice, Manny enrolled at Otis, the L.A. County Art Institute.

"I didn't know one end of the pencil from the other," related Manny, "and I didn't know what art was about when I went there. Fortunately, the beginning classes were booked and they put me temporarily in advanced classes, which accelerated my learning very quickly. I had good teachers who took an interest in me, and I met some painters who said they would teach me. Art school was mostly learning technique, but those four painters expanded my experience and skills. They understood the concepts and how history, politics and philosophy applied to art. After two years, I graduated and started to paint. I couldn't make a living."

That's when Manny moved his family to Santa Cruz and began painting houses and hanging out at the Sticky Wicket. But painting houses didn't provide the support he needed to raise his family. When the new freeway destroyed business at the Sticky Wicket, Manny decided to open his own place, Manuel's Mexican Restaurant in nearby Aptos. He thought he knew how to cook, and he enjoyed it, but he quickly learned that he didn't know the first thing about restaurant cooking. It was an innovative time and Manny's, as the restaurant became known, featured flamenco music, performers and dancers, poetry readings and other free-style events that kept people coming back.

"Gurus were everywhere and the hippie movement was in full blossom," recalled Manny. "I came from a hard-assed world and, all of a sudden, being a hard ass was *verboten*." I was bewildered and in cultural shock. I remember the time this six-foot, five-inch tall guy comes in wearing farmer's overalls and a flower in his hair and grabbed me and kissed me. I thought, 'Oh man! You don't kiss me.' But then I learned you can show affection and friendship. I began to open my eyes and see that a culture was developing around me. There were some wonderful times, as well as some really hard times. I made some mistakes putting my feet where they didn't belong, like in my mouth. In the long run, I think I learned more than the hippies did."

Once, when a longhaired guy in overalls came to the restaurant looking for a job waiting tables, Manny told him he didn't have any openings. Manny thought, "No way in hell would I hire someone who looks like you." The guy left and Manny suddenly felt like someone had kicked him in the stomach. How could I do that? He asked himself. If someone had told Manny that, he would want to kill him. He ran after the guy and offered him a job. The next day when the guy waited on the tables, everyone walked out.

"I thought ah shit, that must be the price you pay for being open minded," Manny laughed. "There were some hard-ass conservatives around here but the community has been good to me. They've given me lots of support, and I did well in the restaurant business."

Manny continued his political activities. He served as a member of the Democratic Central Committee in the county and got involved in farm workers' issues such as housing, rural economic development, work study programs and agricultural cooperatives, including a strawberry co-op. He and his wife, Mary Alice, founded the Central Coast Counties Development

Corporation, CCCDC (called 3C-DC), a non-profit umbrella that supported farm worker activities. Manny became the executive director and helped organize the San Jerardo housing co-op outside Salinas, where farmworkers built their own houses. They built a cooler to handle vegetables from farming co-ops and started the Salinas Agricultural Park from federal funds for economic development. They founded programs to educate farm workers and discovered that if activities are too narrowly focused, they won't bring about the desired change.

"I always thought that if you expect to change society, you have to change the economy," Manny explained. "But I found you also have to change people's spirits. People have to expand their minds so they can learn how to work with each other. We taught people business, such as how to market, but we also taught them how to set up environments that help them develop themselves. This wasn't popular with the Feds, because we also asked for money for cultural development."

His interest in art led him to join a number of community arts boards, including the Cabrillo Music Festival. He became the chairman for five years, and when financial difficulties threatened to close the festival, Manny discovered the problems were both conceptual and financial. The Festival needed to reformulate its purpose; what did they want the festival to be? There were too many other music festivals vying for attendance and Manny didn't think the festival could compete on that level. Instead of treating it as just another concert, he urged a new board of directors to raise money and revitalize the festival as a showcase for young composers and musicians.

"I was lucky," said Manny. "I was working with highly intelligent and motivated people."

At the age of 61, after spending years involved in political, artistic and cultural activities in the community, Manny realized it was time to turn over the business reins to younger people. He spent 35 years making a living, working for the community and neglecting his art. If he wanted to fulfill his dream of becoming an artist, he'd better get started. He began to paint full time. His studio just off West Mission filled with brightly colored canvases. Marble sculptures sat atop pedestals, the smell of paint hung in the air, and classical music resounded against the sheet metal ceiling. When asked to explain what style or tradition he paints in, Manny responded that he didn't worry about style.

"I guess you'd say this stuff is idiosyncratic," he said, waving his hand toward the paintings. "I just let it be and don't try to paint messages. Every painting has something in it; the things that are inside me come out. What the hell is this? Therapy? I'd puke if I thought it was just therapy. If you think about famous artists of the past, and read their letters, you find their real concerns were not about art, but creation of forms to explain their world. To the painter, every painting is a form driving the painter to the next step. Art is based on the challenge of chaos. We can't always make sense of things so we're constantly creating new forms to explain the relationships. Some happen to be beautiful.

"Some people say painting is dead, but so what? People have valued art for a long time; it shows that the activity is legitimate. I keep painting anyway. Who cares? The forms come out on their own when I'm painting. Three months later I begin to read it and it gives me insights into myself. Eventually I see how it applies to everything else, how it fits in, how I fit in with everything."

In explaining the creation of a community in Santa Cruz, Manny didn't feel that people gave enough credit to Watsonville, which played a key role in creating Cabrillo

College and bringing the university to Santa Cruz. If not for a small group of people, such as the Wychoffs, Chamberlains and the Orrs, the university wouldn't exist. The university created an atmosphere in which the uniqueness of the community expressed itself. He found encouragement in the fact that Santa Cruz has the audacity to have its own foreign policy, and not leave it to the federal government.

Although Manny was concerned at some of the changes in the community, like the steep rise in housing prices and the influx of high-tech people from Silicon Valley, he was willing to wait and see if they, or the new technology, would bring new ideas to the community. Such ideas have the potential to save the community by bringing new ways of dealing with social, economic and political issues. For example, the Internet may open communication throughout the world, but he wanted to wait and see who owned it before deciding if it's a benefit or a liability.

"The community attracted many young people with new ideas," said Manny. "They renewed interest in the environment, the land and the political and social spheres. I love this city. Sure there are a lot of petty personal things I don't like, but in general, what some people call wacky I call wonderful. It's the spirit of participation and it's pretty good. Life is split into ying and yang, positive and negative forces, and only by awaking to our sensuousness can we realize the magic of being alive."

Chapter 5: Chez Ray and Sleazy D
by Dean Quarnstrom

In keeping with the 1960's spirit of poking fun at contemporary cultural temples, I've always enjoyed riffin' with hipster friends who used spoken language for mutual play. Ray was a skilled Berkeley punster, and also a partner in the overnight Berkeley dining sensation, Chez Panisse. This game-changing, extremely hip restaurant was instantly recognized as a culinary phenomenon. Its founder, Alice Waters, established a new paradigm in truly fine, organic dining experiences, which became known as the "Nouvelle-California" cuisine. Ray aptly bestowed upon me a nickname that served me well during the evolving the 1970's wonder years. To fully explore the magical powers that this nickname brought to me, I only had to follow Ray's two-step process and then show up at Chez Panisse to reap the bounty of his gift.

Step One:

"Good Afternoon, Chez Panisse…How may I help you?" asked the person answering my phone call.

"Yes, hello, is Mr. Ray available?"

A well-known fact in Berkeley lore is that from its opening day, booking a same-day table in the front, downstairs dining room at Chez Panisse was next to impossible. I'm talking about up to a month's wait for a downstairs table at this popular, exciting gourmet eatery. But I possessed the power of Ray's two-step magical gift:

"May I tell Ray who's calling," asked the receptionist?

Step Two:

Here in lay my secret sauce, two words that guaranteed me a prime dinner table at Chez Panisse, in the downstairs, front dining room that very evening.

"Yes, of course, please tell Mr. Ray that Sleazy Dean is

calling." I was never once disappointed when Ray was working the day I called.

"Just a minute, Mr. Dean," the voice would reply and I was placed on hold until Ray picked up my call.

"Sleazy Dean, my most luminescent of luminaries! However may I assist you at this time?" Ray's greeting to me was always that of a perfect gentleman, host and colleague.

"A romantic table for two, Eight-ish, this evening, if possible," I'd reply.

"Of course! Can you please hold for just a moment while I check…?", as if he's consulting some reservation book close at hand, then always I'd receive the same reply.

"Sleazy Dean, you are confirmed for two. Eight-ish it is then, for this evening! Now, is there anything else I can do for you, and please, don't be shy, my most welcomed and promiscuous good sir?"

"Well, perhaps, yes, there is just one, a simple request only, thank you. And, Mr. Ray, please know that, without a doubt, you are Da' Mo' of all my main men, the 'Creme de la Creme', my friend, and my simple request is only that we would be most honored if you might find a moment to join us, if only to share in my in-deflatable joy with an aperitif or three just after this evening's gastronomic adventures." "Aperitif" was our phone code indicating that I'd also bring a treat of my own, everyone's post-dining favorite, brain-stimulating Bolivian diet supplement, for the table's enjoyment.

"Most assuredly," Ray replied. "Perhaps we might also find a moment to partake in a fine '68 Dom bubbly to honor the pleasure of a visit with my most-favored of guests." And just like that, my evening's glorious, somewhat-mischievous plans were a done deal.

I'd use my privilege only on special occasions, perhaps to impress the current object of my mind's romantic tendencies, knowing full well how positively the "same-day reservation" ploy could impress the current focus of my affection's desires; it almost guaranteed the hoped-for result that would follow later, well after dinner. And Ray was always a man of his word: as soon as I was seated, a hand-painted bottle of Crystal, or a Dom Perignon, would appear at my table.

The fine bubbly was always Ray's treat, and it guaranteed our waiter an excellent tip from me for the uncorking service. What a wonderful time we all shared during those fine meals and all because Ray and I had become trusted friends while doing business with one another. I was a source for a variety of desired "specialty" items, including worthy used cars, good weed and the occasional pleasure of high-quality cocaine, my gift to our dinner conversation and enjoyment, no matter how one's appetite might suffer, and a pleasurable foreplay to the even grander thrills in store for later that evening.

Why did I sell used cars, when I was already gainfully engaged in driving loads of weed up and down the Eastern Seaboard, and making good money? Simply because I loved cars, especially the vintage 1940's and '50's regal road beauties that were still coming up for sale. In the Midwest, where I'd gotten into cars as a kid, most of the older Detroit creations had long since rusted away from the salted winter roads, and were beyond salvage. But in California's dry and warmer climate, they could still be seen on the roads everywhere, and usually in pristine condition; when sold, they went for almost no money at all. The owners were dying off and their inheritors too modern to appreciate the flowing lines and design of these older "ladies of the night."

Before I fell into the car hustling business, I'd already been the proud owner of three 1949 Oldsmobile 2-door Coupes, a 1950 dark green Olds Fastback with a factory sun-visor, and a 1947 Olds 2-door Coupe, in which I delivered my first Acid deals to Seattle and Vancouver, followed by a trunk load of Weed to Chicago, before selling the car to Prankster Pat, who put another 50,000 miles on the gem before she died. Neal Cassady remembered me as "Dean with the '47 Olds Coupe," which he'd always claimed was one of his favorite road-trip cars.

These huge, heavy and voluptuously-styled early American GM products were marvelous to sit and ride in, watching the scenery pass by, looking over and beyond its long, full-bodied hood. It was like driving a well-endowed lover with generous soft cloth cushions to firmly hold and guide you on the journey, such graceful, lovely sculpted lines extending forward to the large, full headlamps that sought to illuminate one's night-time adventures. The enameled metal dashboards were pleasing to the eye, accentuated with chrome trim and numerous faux-ivory knobs to control the car's interior functions in elegant style. I also drove a '47 Cadillac crème-colored convertible, with rolled red leather seats, which could comfortably seat eight people before the days of mandatory seatbelts. I gave it to a musician friend from Chicago, Nick, who, soon afterwards, I'm told, parked it in the north Sausalito mud-flats surrounding The Quicksilver Messenger's rehearsal studio. It's probably still there, buried under 10 feet of mud and ocean water.

I sometimes used my '59, lime-green Porsche 356 convertible, the first with roll-up side windows, to deliver Acid-soaked aspirin tablets around the Bay area, with Skyline Blvd. my preferred route for driving fast in the world's second most beautiful, open-air roadster. And before this, in 1963, I bought my first, used VW cloth-top, 23-window van in Chicago, and drove my first wife to San Francisco across the Northern U.S; it was one of many VW's I'd own over the coming 20 years, and the only vehicle that almost killed me. Having a wide selection of cars to choose from was an affordable hobby to pursue back in the day.

As I grew more passionate about the world of cars, and the art of buying and selling these Masters of The Universe, the East Bay provided the best access to a wonderful supply of every sort of used vehicle one could imagine, from every country on earth. I'd been seriously into cars long before I could legally drive them.

Mine was the first generation of Americans to take full advantage of the great new Interstate Highway System being carved into every part of America's landscape, at a time when gas was twenty-eight cents a gallon, older used cars were cheap and plentiful, and our country was a wide open canvas for the youth to explore; and explore we did. A three-day drive from San Francisco to Chicago might cost $50, and a pound of weed cost $100 and sold for up to four times as much, so ten pounds meant a sizeable profit for a few days of driving. Bart The Fart paid me $10 a pound to deliver loads from Miami to D.C., Atlanta, Chicago, or New York. A rented Chrysler's trunk would hold 600 pounds, and I enjoyed making this drive many times a year, for many years. Great road cars were available in Miami in the spring each year, needing to be driven north for their elderly, cold-climate-avoiding owners, who'd driven them south to Miami for the winter months, but couldn't be bothered to make the return drive. I'd often drive a new Cadillac or Lincoln to New York or New Jersey for the owner from Miami, after filling the car's trunk with as many pounds of weed as it would hold.

Beginning in 1966, based out of Berkeley and Santa Cruz, I moved up the seniority ranks to become a major player in a small Berkeley group of hip, used car traders, working the large market of student buyers always looking for affordable used cars. We facetiously called ourselves "Car Hustlers."

I'd put Chez Panisse's Ray in a fine used vehicle for a very low price, and he reciprocated with my special arrangement at his restaurant. It was a unique, short-lived period in the late 60's through mid 70's in California, when a gigantic loophole existed in California's DMV rules, which was summarily exploited.

Our band of car hustlers were fierce competitors, each hoping to be the first to find and buy every suitable used car that appeared on the local market. We'd learned how to maximize any car's resale profit by abusing the lax enforcement of California's DMV regulations.

The law vaguely didn't not allow the first car buyer to pass on a car's title to a second buyer without first recording the sale with the DMV, thereby potentially bypassing the cumbersome and costly DMV fees and paper trail bureaucracy. Our love of all-things-motorized, and our free-wheeling lifestyles, meant we were probably crooks in actual deed and the eyes of the law, but all of this was also unclear, and our code was "Ignore Alien Orders", and the services we provided earned us the respect, even a certain heroic status, from our generation's buyers.

We scooped up the wide variety of used cars that local people needed to sell, couldn't afford to repair, or just wanted to be rid of. We then resold the same vehicles, many needing only minor repairs, to anyone looking for affordable new wheels. We took great pride in our skilled navigation of the DMV's poorly-implemented code, which often proved quite beneficial to all involved in a car transaction. The sellers might be thrilled to finally be free of that hunk of junk, that unavoidable eyesore, just sitting there in the driveway; the new buyer's needed to find a good, affordable car to drive, no matter if it was still registered in the former owner's name; and we car hustler desired to quickly pass along a working vehicle for a handsome profit with no paper trail leading back to us.

I took pride in developing finely-honed, sales-related negotiating skills that served me well in life. Usually, it was a student I was buying from, longing to be freed from the hated gift, filled with so many years of unwanted childhood memories, the 10-year-old, family station wagon; or the car for sale was associated with hoping-to-be-forgotten events, or painful memories of a past situation that I'd look for, try to pry out, to sense or feel and as subtly as possible, dig into, work to bring out, probe at ever so gently, and use solely to get the seller to lower their asking price. And so, if ten minutes of mind- gaming a seller could lead to the purchase of a used Ford station wagon with good tires, advertised for $400, for just $70, I won. Then, if I could sell this same Ford wagon for $700 within an hour to a buyer who would drive it hard for a few months, up until the current registration expired, this vehicle was solid gold. It was potentially worth thousands of dollars to the buyer, especially if the buyer was a frequent visitor to San Francisco, a city notorious for its expensive parking tickets.

The Ford's buyer could flagrantly park in red zones, bus zones, loading zones — anywhere parking was illegal throughout the Bay Area because the new buyer simply hadn't bothered to register the car in his own name. Any new parking citations were charged to registered owner of record, or the unknown seller. I was the middle man, separating the two, and the new buyer was really the law-breaker, and also very much appreciated the car hustler's services.

In a tiny way, my small gift to Ray and his partners helped them to realize their passion for great food: the time and money saved by Ray's healthy collection of unpaid parking citations contributed in a some way to the creation of today's vital environmental awareness, and to the growth of the organic farming movement, which took roots in the Chez Panisse cuisine, and the garden-to-table, California-grown 1960's lifestyle that supported it. The whole situation also informed my own convoluted moral stance on how I earned a living.

The DMV's loophole had been artfully exploited, with no real ethical considerations of potential outcomes ever mentioned by even one car hustler working in Berkeley and North Oakland. We were having too much fun, and making great money to boot. The comedic competition between us was hilarious, the extents to which one might go to beat out the other buyers for each used car that came up for sale, and for the lowest possible price, became wild, very enjoyable street theatre for a few of us.

I was a silent partner in an auto repair garage in Berkeley, owned by two friends, who both loved automobiles. Tony Ducati (a motorcycle racer on weekends) was the Chief Wrench, the ace mechanic of the business, and my go-to advisor. When a particular used car owner needed extra convincing that the vehicle up for sale was worth much less than the current asking price, I'd hire Tony for an hour to accompany me to inspect the car, to act as my testing expert. His day job repairing older vehicles often left him covered in oily grease, so he usually looked like a mechanic. He had no problem crawling under the car I was wanting to buy, and grabbing hold of, say, a greasy tie rod arm, or shock absorber, anything he could get his hands around, and shake it side to side, up and down, supposedly checking out the car for any problems.

Needless to say, Tony always found something wrong with the car, often doing his thing in the dark, oily underside of the used car. He'd find some grease or congealed engine goo and smear the oily mess on his face and arms, all the while grunting and groaning during his inspection. Then, at the most appropriate moment, he'd emerge from under the beast, streaked head to toe with oil and dirt, popping out just at the moment I was telling the seller how much I really wanted to get this car. Tony would jump to his feet, mumbling "…piece of shit, dude, needs a total suspension rebuild, new tie rod ends and ball joints at the minimum, and probably new brakes all around…", or something equally devastating. I'd be crestfallen, so deeply disappointed. We were performing a classic Mutt and Jeff Routine for the owner. I'd argue on behalf of the car's good features while Tony'd tell me I was out of my fucking mind. We'd go back and forth, maybe up to 5 minutes of good theater, intended only to get the owner to lower the asking price.

See, we knew that people usually only sold their cars when they were already convinced that the once-costly, valuable vehicle was now on its last legs and could blow up at any minute. They knew, deep down, that the car they were selling wasn't worth anywhere even near their original, only hoped for asking price. Often, even before Tony and I had reached the planned-for time to stop arguing back and forth, the seller would interrupt us, feeling like a piece of shit for trying to unload this worthless clunker onto some unsuspecting fool at any price — in their hearts, they were sure that this used car would soon cause the buyer a shitload of trouble, and were prematurely having seller's remorse — and just ask me what I'd pay for it. Wham, Bam, it worked!

And if this didn't happen, then, when it felt like the time was right, maybe after a good ten minutes of our back and forth arguing about the car, I would stop, turn to the owner and make a ridiculously low, cash offer for the car of my dreams. I might say "…just in love with this model, I do want it, and hell, I'm willing to pay whatever it costs to get it back in shape again. Will you take (my very low offer) right now?" And then, not another word from either Tony or me. And nine out of ten times, the owner would accept my offer, and we all could walk away feeling quite pleased within.

That's how the hustle went, and usually a newly purchased used car needed only minor repairs to raise its resale value up to ten times more than the price I'd paid for it. Occasionally, there was nothing wrong at all, and the car could be flipped within the hour to the next buyer. I'd pay Tony $100 for his help, and pay him again to actually fix whatever needed fixing. I could still make good money without charging the excessive prices that the greedy licensed used car dealers and repair shops gouged from their buying public.

Cal-Berkeley students became my prime source for used cars; they usually had school work on their minds when it came time to sell their clunker or buy one. When it was obvious that a student seller's next fantasy dream ride was a classy new Mustang or a stylish Camero muscle car, my ruse as buyer became much easier: the more repair issues I could point out with the car they were selling, the easier it was for the naive student seller to justify taking next to nothing for the car, if only to be rid of the memories it brought back of those boring, middle-class, backseat outings into Nature with Mommy and Dad. I once paid $70 for a like-new, pristine Buick Vista Cruiser, which could sleep two adults in sublime comfort and safely out of any bad weather, or could hold in the rear bed most everything that three or four hippies would need to live for a year. The Vista Cruiser would easily fetch $800 after I'd spent $40 on two new shocks, and steam-cleaned the engine to its original factory-clean appearance, an excellent profit for an excellent car. I mean, you could fold down the rear seat, drop some Acid, lie back and stretch out while watching the passing cloud-movie above through the rear's elegant, back-seat overhead skylight.

If a VW Bug needed major engine repairs, I'd pay up to $80 for one in otherwise great shape. Tony could remove the VW's engine, rebuild the entire motor, and re-install the new motor in under four hours and $125 for the engine parts. With a new motor, the same VW would quickly sell for $1,200, meaning Tony and I would split up to $1,000 for one day's investment. VW's were the car hustler's dream vehicle, easy to repair and easier to resell. When a hustler was the first to spot a hand-written used-car-for-sale ad posted on one of Berkeley's three top community-accessed bulletin boards, he'd quickly remove and pocket the ad, for personal follow-up only.

Tony's garage specialized in foreign and sport car repairs, and at one point I ended up buying three Jaguar XK-120 Roadsters from Tony's customers. Jags were expensive to drive and constantly needed repairs, but were the embodiment of a pure esthetic form of art to an avid auto enthusiast, their voluptuous curves flowing forward from the broad windscreen to the sculpted headlamps, all their lines just pleasing to the driver's eye, as seen looking out through the large thin steering wheel, a wonder to ponder while moving at high speed. And under the hood, such elegance to be found in the smooth, highly-polished engine metal parts and covers, almost silken to the touch, and the bright-metal Solex carburetors, reflecting asymmetric shards of sunlight back to your eyes. There were so many knobs and toggle-switches just to fiddle, to play with.

Driving a British Red Jaguar XK120 Roadster was the perfect metaphor for the experience of holding, caressing a beautiful woman with your hands and eyes. And these ladies were quite fickle to boot; in my own experience it took at least two additional XK120's on hand, for the access to their irregular Wentworth-sized British auto parts, to be harvested as needed, just to keep the third one, your one and only true love, running and on the road. I spent maybe $800 for all three: the red roadster I kept repaired just for the pure pleasure of being in the company of such a delicate beauty on the occasional motoring jaunt around town.

   A British red Jaguar roadster was a real eye-catcher, drew attention to the driver, and for this reason alone, I had to finally end our relationship. Today the three cars together are worth $800,000 or more; back in the day, I sold all three to a single buyer for $2,200, still a nice profit after having enjoyed the intimate pleasures of a glorious love affair with this red goddess during one, timeless summer. I used the sale's proceeds to purchase the more exotic younger sister to the XK120, an XKE Coupe, Jag's revered sports model designed to drive on the new highways. But this lovely came with an endemic sadness too, which I experienced first-hand. The XKEs were designed with a tragic design flaw, its cooling system. The radiator was just too small and too fragile to cool the car's powerful engine, rendering the car useless for any serious, long-term driving fun. I was fortunate, and sold the beauty to a Jaguar enthusiast for $4,500.

   My Berkeley Jaguar collector and mentor, Michael D, asked me to go in 50/50 with him on the purchase-for-resale of a very exotic, hand-built British road-racing car. Michael was ill with Hodgkin's disease, which left him very weak, and he needed help to finalize the sale and transfer of this racing car to a buyer waiting for its delivery back in England. The Lister Corvette was an all-aluminum, fuel-injected Chevy Corvette V8-powered stick of road dynamite, a coveted British road-racing machine. Its ultra-light, hand-formed, bright aluminum body was mounted over a narrow, tubular steel frame, similar in appearance to the infamous Jaguar D-model racing champion; both were low-to-the-ground, sleek rockets on four wheels, with seating for only the driver. This Lister model was one of only five produced in England.

Since arriving in California, the Lister had been stored off the ground on four jacks (or perhaps hidden) in a garage behind a family home just north of Berkeley. I could have bought this beauty myself from Michael for $4,000, no problem, but I passed it by. Ah…, looking back, it was just one of many, "if only I'd…" missed opportunities in my life. If only I'd had the brains and foresight to buy it for beans back then. But I'd never been taught or ever learned about the world of investing, how to think about putting money into items that actually increased in value over time. Today the Lister would easily fetch up to $2 Million.

Michael's buyer in England planned to race the Lister, and all I did to double my cash investment was to load and trailer the Lister from Berkeley to the Port of Oakland shipping harbor. It was so light that I pushed it by myself into a waiting freight container. Unfortunately, I later learned, the very first time the new owner tested it on a race track, he'd immediately lost control, crashed and was killed, also demolishing the Lister.

Hustling cars was great fun, but, as with most good things, there was a downside with consequences that we hadn't considered while in the thick of doing business. And when I finally realized the financial damage that our DMV shenanigans had caused a few of the sellers I'd bought cars from, I quit the business almost overnight. Almost a year after selling a fine station wagon to a close friend, Marc called to tell me an interesting tale of what he'd just experienced regarding this vehicle.

While crossing the Bay Bridge from his waterbed store in San Francisco, Marc had heard the unfortunate story of a used car seller being interviewed on a radio talk show, telling the listening audience about an incredible legal problem he faced regarding the sale of his family's station wagon. The owner had neglected to inform the DMV of the change of ownership when he'd sold a car, which he then described in detail; the make, model, year, color of the very car Marc was driving at that very moment. This seller had never asked for, and didn't know the name of the young man to whom he'd sold the car, which was me. As a result of this slight oversight in the official DMV protocol, the seller's handing over the title to his wagon without notifying the DMV of the buyer's name, all legal responsibility for the car still remained with the seller, including the more than $30,000 racked up in unpaid parking tickets in San Francisco alone, with many thousands of dollars more in parking fines owed throughout the Bay Area. This man's problems led the state lawmakers to swiftly close this DMV loophole, basically ending our cozy little car hustling business at the same time.

After hearing the unfortunate story, including a detailed description of his car, Marc took the first freeway exit on 80 East in Emeryville, parked the guilty vehicle on the first side street he came upon, and walked away, after clearing out anything he could find with his name on it, leaving the doors unlocked and the key in the ignition. He called me later, and we briefly enjoyed the ironic humor of the story about the car, and our good fortune at not being identified as the culprits.

"Sleazy Dean, please, the evening's on me tonight and my deepest thanks for another lovely evening," Ray said as we rose from the table and warmly embraced our goodbyes.

I never abused, and always enjoyed the wondrous gifts and new people that came my way through my business. What a marvelous, exciting, and rewarding time of life we all shared, being participants in that emerging 1960's underground subculture that blossomed and spread outward from the San

Francisco Bay Area. I truly enjoyed it all, while somehow usually knowing not to abuse the trusts and privileges that came my way. At the same time, I don't know how, I almost always knew when enough was good enough, and when it was probably time to just move on, and to keep on movin' on.

Chapter 6: The William James Association Prison Arts Project
Jack Bowers

The William James Association Prison Arts Project, and the Arts in Corrections program which it spawned, have strong roots in the Santa Cruz community, and at UCSC in particular. In its unique vision of the role that the fine arts can play in social justice, the Prison Arts Project reflects the values of service and innovation that characterized UCSC's early years, and that still inspire many in our community. Thriving once again since its revival in 2014, Arts in Corrections continues to provide a model for how the arts can contribute to a community in truly substantial ways.

For over forty years, California's finest artists have brought their creativity and craft into California prisons: to teach, to inspire, and to create space in which men and women whose lives have been damaged by behavior and circumstance can discover that they have something to contribute to their world, and that they can find in themselves the artist, the actor, the musician or the poet, rather than the addict, the failure, the criminal. Research shows that beyond its direct artistic benefit, prison arts programs promote socialization, improved family relationships, motivation towards self improvement and reductions in recidivism and disciplinary actions.

The formation of the William James Association in 1973 by Page Smith and Paul Lee provided the base from which the Prison Arts Project grew. [Discussion of the early days of the William James Association is covered in an earlier volume of Hip Santa Cruz]. It should be noted that, from its outset, the WJA board had a substantial component of practicing artists: Roy Rydell, Frances Rydell, Al Johnsen, Mary Holmes and, indeed, Page Smith himself.

Precedent for the Prison Arts Project exists in the work of UCSC History of Consciousness graduate student, Karlene Faith. In the 70s, as part of her graduate work, Karlene taught a course at Soledad prison that included prisoners and UCSC undergraduates. Her book "Soledad, University of the Poor" documented that work. From there she formed the Santa Cruz Women's Prison Project, which for two years brought distinguished teachers to the California Institution for Women in Frontera. The on campus presence during the 70s of Black Panther Huey Newton, another History of Consciousness graduate student, clearly created a context in which incarceration and the gross social inequities in our society were a part of the campus conversation.

Eloise Pickard Smith, Page Smith's wife, and a distinguished artist herself, was appointed to the first California Arts Council in 1976 by Governor Jerry Brown, along with Ruth Asawa, Noah Purifoy and Peter Coyote. As these members of the arts council toured the state to assess the state of the arts in California, Eloise discovered an arts community in the California Medical Facility, a prison in Vacaville. An inmate-led Arts Guild and Performing Musicians Guild demonstrated that the arts were alive even in the depths of our prisons. To nurture this community of artists, Eloise resigned her position on the Arts Council, and used the William James Association as a non-profit channel to collect funding for the nascent Prison Arts Project. Eloise's partner in this work was a visual artist, musician and prisoner at Vacaville, Vern McKee. Vern said of Eloise, "Without Eloise there would be no program at all. If I had looked inside the [prison] walls and found the need and hunger for this program, Eloise looked outside and into the future and the strength, courage and wisdom to give it life and make it grow."

Eloise based her concept of a prison arts program on

the work of potter and poet, M. C. Richards. In her book "Centering" Richards put forward the idea that "all the arts we practice are apprenticeship. The big art is our life." This was certainly a solid foundation for a prison arts program. During the early years of prison arts at Vacaville, under Eloise's direction, ceramics and writing were the two art forms that were taught, drawing very directly on Richards' philosophy. To Eloise the goal of prison arts was "to provide an opportunity where a man can gain the satisfaction of creation rather than destruction, earn the respect of his fellows, and gain recognition from family and outsiders."

The William James Board enthusiastically supported Eloise's work. Page Smith said "the true task of the artist is to discover her or his relationship to a community, a community often in desperate need of the artist's power to see the world anew… artists discover through these communities how serious and essential their arts are, that art is not a matter of critics and shows and salons but of endurance and survival." Or, as James Baldwin so succinctly puts it, "what artists and prisoners have in common is that both know what it means to be free."

There were two other corners of the tripod on which Eloise constructed the Prison Arts Project. She insisted that the program use the finest possible artists — it was through them that the fierce commitment to excellence and self-discipline would be most apparent to the student. Even as Arts in Corrections grew to a state wide program, Eloise continued to advocate that the artists in the program be chosen first for the quality of their art. Among the many great artists who taught in the program were national poet laureate Juan Felipe Herrera and National Heritage Fellow Agustin Lira.

The third corner of the tripod was a realistic view of the politics of a prison arts program. Providing art to felons is not always an easy sell, and to gain the necessary support at the state level, it required a politician of both vision and power. This came in the form of State Senator Henry Mello of Watsonville, who became a tireless advocate for Arts in Corrections. In 1980, he authored the legislation that first brought Arts in Corrections into six state prisons. Until his retirement in 1992, Mello championed Arts in Corrections, insisting that it be expanded to the new prisons California was building as a part of the increasingly militant "tough on crime" movement, and defending it against those within the Department of Corrections who felt that there was no place for an arts program in a prison.

In 1980, at Eloise's invitation, I began teaching songwriting and music at Soledad Prison. I had formed the Santa Cruz Songwriters Guild in 1978 to promote and educate local songwriters. We had aligned ourselves with William James as a fiscal sponsor, so they were aware of the work I was doing. At a meeting in the Warden's office with Eloise, myself, Warden Reginald Pulley and the then artist facilitator, Pacific Grove muralist Dick Crispo discussed how we might begin a music program. Two weeks later distinguished jazz artist Andrew Hill and I were escorted through two sallyports, a locked door and another barred gate to meet with about 40 musicians in an empty gymnasium. As we sat in a circle and talked with the men, it became clear that there were already musicians there, and that they were thirsty for knowledge, support and a sense of connection with the outside. For the musicians and would be musicians of Soledad, it was an incredible exciting prospect to think that they would connect with and learn from musicians from "the streets." For Andrew and me it was life affirming to discover such an eager audience, and feel how these men valued art not just as entertainment but as a source of light in their foreboding world.

Over the next two years, Andrew and I worked to establish

classes, acquire music equipment and find space for the prisoner musicians of Soledad. Andrew had begun this work at a slow point in his musical life, and left the program in 1982 to resume his international performance and composition career. With the invaluable support of Los Angeles jazz musician and arranger Buddy Harper, I went on to become the music teacher at Soledad, and, one year later, I took over the position of Artist Facilitator for the Arts in Corrections program from Dick Crispo.

I worked at Soledad prison for twenty five years, teaching music, organizing band programs and facilitating classes in the arts. To leave Santa Cruz five mornings a week and drive to a prison of 5,000 inmates set in the middle of the lettuce fields of Salinas Valley was a mind altering experience, to say the least. Where Santa Cruz was about as loose and permissive a culture as we had in our country, the prison was rigid, adversarial and vibrating with the constant threat of violence. I had to learn how to exist in this almost feudal society, to learn to be consistent and fair, to listen and respond and also set clear expectations. It challenged me in ways that I could not have imagined.

Woody Allen's maxim about 80% of life is showing up definitely held true at the prison. Neither the prisoners nor the correctional staff accept newcomers easily. There is an inherent distrust that here is another "do-gooder" who will just mess things up. The prisoner looks on the newcomer as someone to take advantage of; the correctional officer sees someone who will make their life more difficult. After a few years, I found that most people in the prison accepted me and the Arts in Corrections program. They learned that I was reliable, and that if I said I would do something, in most cases I would. To their surprise, I think, the officers learned that the men in Arts in Corrections classes were more interested in practicing their art than creating problems. Their fellow inmates learned that the guy in the cell next door, whatever his race or gang affiliation, was a good artist and respected him for that.

Soledad Prison, or the Correctional Training Facility as it was officially known, was built in the 50s when Earl Warren was Governor of California. Its construction and programs reflected the rehabilitative philosophy of that era, which held that prisoners who learned a viable vocation would leave prison and use the skills they'd learned to get a good job and offend no more. The prison was divided into three facilities, Central, North and South, and we provided programs to each facility. This meant that I was pretty busy most of the time. If I had a break at Central I would run down to South to resupply the band room with drumsticks and guitar strings. I would use my office time to make sure that the Art Class at North had enough students, check on the progress of a memo for an art exhibit, or talk to a Lieutenant about the next yard show.

Dick Crispo had already laid the foundation for a strong fine arts program at Soledad. The quarter mile long Central Corridor was the site of his mural, the world's longest indoor mural. The music program that we developed at Soledad acknowledged the talent and skills of the resident musicians with a vibrant band program. At any one time, anywhere between 15 and 25 different inmate bands rehearsed and performed regularly at the institution. They took advantage of four established rehearsal rooms with a full complement of music equipment — drums, amps, guitars, PA, etc. A couple of "honors" bands of skilled musicians studied jazz repertoire and improvisation with my direction, but also very much as a cooperative enterprise. To my surprise, a 12 week music theory class I began teaching became incredibly popular, to the point that I taught it almost continuously for my last ten years at the prison.

One of the most oppressive parts of prison is boredom — the same food, the same people, the same stories, the same cellmate, etc. In its own way, Arts in Corrections helped alleviate that. During the summer, we would hold music performances on the Recreation Yards. It was always a special day for us. Early Saturday morning, I would meet the musicians in the Band Room. We would load the music equipment on five or six ungainly laundry carts and head down the corridor, through the West Gate metal detectors and out onto the Yard. The stage was set against the 12 foot high fence, topped with razor wire. Once upon a time the stage had been the boxing ring, until boxing was eliminated from the Recreation program. It usually took an hour or so to get things set up, so we would start playing around 9:30, assuming there were no alarms, or late releases, or fog counts, or escape details, or late feedings, or anything else from the infinite list of what could cancel program.

Usually three of four bands would perform, unless it was a special holiday like Cinco de Mayo or Juneteenth. As the various bands began playing, the audience in front of the stage would rotate, mostly Mexicans for the Norteño band, mostly white for the rock band, and mostly Black for the R & B band. If the music was particularly rhythmic, some of the men would start to dance. I will never forget watching Mexican inmates dancing as we played a Cumbia. You could see the guard towers and the fences fall away as they were transported back to a park in San Jose or a niece's quinceñera. We also had a jazz band, drawn from the best musicians in the facility. This band was integrated, so it would draw a mixed crowd of music aficionados.

The leadership of Arts in Corrections in Sacramento expected that the program would serve all the arts, so in addition to our music program, we had weekly classes in visual arts and writing at two or three different sites. Each of these classes required space, equipment, supplies and students. Managing a program of this scope was more than one individual could accomplish, so we relied on a crew of dedicated inmate workers to keep up with all this. They maintained student lists, typed memos, managed the rehearsal rooms and interfaced with correctional staff. Frequently artists themselves, they were the heart and soul of the Arts in Corrections program.

It would be an oversight not to mention the importance that racial politics play in prison life. Everyone, prisoners and staff alike, is constantly measuring what their group receives against others. The consequence of this is that one must strive to be absolutely fair and inclusive in all things. Each of our classes would be racially balanced. The band program would be composed of Mexican, Black and White bands. The prisoners who worked in the program would represent the major ethnic groups of the prison. In our jazz band, we found a perfect intersection by playing Latin Jazz, it appealed to everyone. Because of this, and the value that the entire prison population found in Arts in Corrections, the rooms where we rehearsed and taught were considered off limits for most types of illegal activity. I learned this after my retirement from one of the men who had been a mainstay of the program for many years. He now serves of the William James Association Board of Directors.

Santa Cruz provided a rich source of artists and support for the program at Soledad. The fact that the William James Association was based in Santa Cruz also meant that Soledad benefitted frequently from visiting artists and special programs. Page and Eloise's daughter, Ellen Gruys Davidson, was the first manager of the Prison Arts Project.

As such, she established many of the policies and procedures that the program followed as it grew. Without her daily work protecting and nurturing the artists and program in those early years, Arts in Corrections would surely have not succeeded to the extent that it did. After her retirement, Laurie Brooks took over as Executive Director and has done superb work managing the program through many difficult times.

Victoria Sulski taught visual arts at Soledad prison for over 10 years. An MFA graduate student of Betty Edwards, author of Drawing from the Right Side of the Brain, Victoria established a disciplined, structured class that nurtured many fine artists. Claire Braz-Valentine taught Creative Writing at Soledad, San Quentin and Central California Women's Facility for almost twenty years. Her play, "Women Behind Bars," co-written with her students at CCWF, has been performed throughout California, on both sides of the prison fence. More recently she helped establish a new writing program at High Desert State Prison in Susanville.

Guillermo Aranda, Watsonville muralist, first joined the arts program at Soledad prison through the recommendation of Eduardo Carrillo of UCSC. Teaching through both the William James Association and as a California Arts Council Artist-in-Residence, "Yermo" taught many artists, and produced murals of great spiritual and artistic beauty. When Arts in Corrections returned in 2015, Yermo returned to teach for two years. His class produced a mural that is in the Visiting Room at Salinas Valley State Prison.

Nigel Sanders-Self was a young actor with Shakespeare Santa Cruz when he was recruited to teach theater at Soledad. He expected great things from his students and was not disappointed. His productions of "Zoo Story", Eugene O'Neill's "In the Zone," Jean Genet's "The Maids" and other plays contributed greatly to the growing respect for Arts in Corrections in both the prison community and the artistic community outside.

Barrington McLean, Visual artist and sculptor, was an inspiring teacher at Soledad, working in both two dimensional and three dimensional mediums. After the demise of Arts in Corrections in 2003, his students used his personalized, Socratic methods to continue arts classes on their own. Barrington also went on to establish an Arts in Corrections program at Wasco State Prison.

Kenny Hill was recruited to teach classical guitar at Soledad based on strong student interest. Kenny used his luthiery experience to assist a student in building a guitar kit. This led to discussion of the possibility of building more guitars. A unique partnership between the vocational mill and cabinet program and Arts in Corrections, supported by California Arts Council grant, led to a three year luthiery project, where students produced fine classical guitars for music programs in Salinas Valley schools. Curiously, it was this experience that led Kenny to form Hill Guitar Company. In addition to building fine guitars, Hill Guitars has also introduced construction innovations that have advanced the technology of this ancient craft.

Santa Cruz singer/songwriter Lacy J Dalton, aka Jill Croston, performed benefit concerts at Soledad Prison and at San Quentin during the 80s. In 2015, she was recruited to teach guitar and songwriting at High Desert State Prison in Susanville, near her new home in Reno. Through her national reputation and amazing people skills, Lacy helped establish credibility and support for an arts program in a prison notorious for its resistance to inmate programs.

Roberta Ruiz was an MFA graduate of Stanford who brought intense energy and vision to her teaching at Soledad.

Working in the protective housing units with gang drop outs and others with unique criminal histories, she taught art as first and foremost a process, not a product. She organized a powerful exhibit that toured Stanford, San Jose State University and UCSC. The centerpiece of the exhibit was a full scale mockup of a Soledad cell constructed of the paperboard boxes in which prisoners received their lunch. Decorated with everything from self-portraits to domino scores, this amazing installation showed both the fine work of her students and graphically conveyed the environment from which this work came.

Eric Thierman was recruited to document the program during its early years. His video "Art and the Prison Crisis" helped establish credibility for Arts in Corrections by bringing the experience of making art in prison to a large audience.

Ken Arconti, accomplished blues guitarist and songwriter, taught blues guitar and blues ensemble at both the first Soledad prison (CTF) and at Salinas Valley State Prison, which opened in the early 90s as California's prison population exploded. Ken was beloved by his students for his musical skill and his knowledge of the blues heritage.

Steve Wiesinger was the first writing teacher at Soledad. He was one of the pioneers whose integrity and consistency helped bring the program respect. Jeff Arnetti taught creative writing and poetry at Soledad for 3 years. He put together an anthology of student writing that skillfully combined the doggerel poetry tradition that existed at the prison with more modern free verse.

Although being the only full time representative of Arts in Corrections at the prison was a demanding and sometimes very lonely job, the community of artists working in the program throughout the state was a supportive counterbalance for me. By the 90s, there were thirty full time artist facilitators around the state, as well as literally hundreds of teaching artists. They were a great resource for problem solving, new ideas, or successful tactics to bring projects to fruition. More than anything though, this far flung community allowed us to feel like a movement, a cadre of dedicated artists who were working to bring change to California's prisons through the healing power of the arts. I remember fondly reaching out to Graham Moody, the artist facilitator at Pelican Bay State Prison on a Wednesday evening as I sat in my office doing paperwork. I remember the joy we felt at the annual Arts in Corrections conference, where we shared successes and failures and dreamed of a prison full of artists or of an Arts in Corrections branch that would support our students through the difficult task of parole, where we passed on recommendations of exemplary students who were being transferred to another prison, and returned to our dreams and a revitalized sense of purpose.

It bears mentioning that Arts in Corrections was, in the end, at least as much a creation of its students as of its teachers. Our students inspired us by their dedication to their craft and their hard work; they opened themselves up as individuals and as members of the disparate groups in the prison to become an integrated class, or a band, or a mural crew. Almost without our knowledge, they made sure that the class was a safe space for the teacher and for the other students. Over the years I became very close with some of the men I worked with. We would spend many hours together each week. In a prison society marked by extreme territoriality and rigid gang rules, they stood out as individuals who lived by their integrity and strength of character. There is no doubt in my mind that, in the end, any success of the Arts in Corrections program in California prisons was built on their recognition that this was a valuable program for them and their community. It was, and continues to be, an honor to work with them.

Epilogue: Arts in Corrections had its funding withdrawn in 2003, bringing the program to a sudden, disturbing halt. However, through the dedication of a small cadre of artists, the heritage of the program was preserved at three prisons: San Quentin and prisons near Sacramento and Los Angeles. In 2012, with attitudes about incarceration changing, and the recognition of the deeply imbedded racism in our criminal justice system, the political climate became ripe for the revival of the program. A working group composed of California Lawyers for the Arts, the William James Association, and Tim Robbin's Actors Gang worked with sympathetic members of the Legislature to hold hearings on the value of prison arts, and lobby for its restoration. At the same time, the Department of Corrections and Rehabilitation [this last verbal redundancy added by Arnold Schwarzenegger] was under increasing pressure from federal courts to provide leisure time programs in the context of improved mental health. In 2013, this effort led to Arts in Corrections pilot projects at several prisons. The positive response to this work led over the next several years to the full restoration of Arts in Corrections to all 35 California prisons.

Chapter 7: My Transcendental Hero: Jerry Kamstra and the Creative Lineage of Santa Cruz
by Daniel Yaryan

American novelist Jerry Kamstra once wrote, "There are two Henry's I adore, Henry Miller and Henry Thoreau. One taught me to march to my own drum — the other one taught me to say yes to the sun." Such words describe the free-spirited nature of Kamstra and the essence of the Santa Cruz of my childhood.

Even though I didn't meet Jerry until 2010, my memories of growing up in Santa Cruz during the '70s and '80s now intertwine with a parallel existence lived by Kamstra. When I recall riding my bike over the large dirt jumps of the once vacant corner lot next to Batish's India Bazaar, I now think of Jerry buying incense there, digging the sounds of a Sitar. When revisiting the old Mellis Market in my mind — carrying a note from my mom to pick up a six pack of Lone Star beer and a carton of cigarettes with a comic book thrown in — I think of Jerry driving past the Market in his Volkswagen van along Mission Street, then taking a quick right down the steep Laurel hill to downtown.

I'll never forget all those bike rides on West Cliff drive, including checking out the impromptu nudist beach below the pyramidal steel statue. Down my brain corridor, I wonder if Jerry was one of those dudes hanging loose with all the beautiful women on the beach that we peered at through the ice plants, excitedly marveling at their anatomical glory. I said yes to the solar rays in Santa Cruz and the bounty of flesh-energy and independence it brought. I also marched to my own backbeat, just as Kamstra and other deep thinkers did before him. Back in the bygone days, humans were more contemplative, unhindered by the constructs of real estate and unrestrained by stellar costs to move — and be moved — like nowadays.

I lament all the long-gone landmark places once adorning downtown Santa Cruz and the nearby reaches of the county and think of Jerry Kamstra being there before, after or at the same time as I was — even though I didn't know him yet — intersecting pieces of my Santa Cruz past.

Many times, I locked up my bike next to the pretzel stand in front of Cooper House and entered the historic building as the tunes of Warmth, other musicians and community sounds resonated in my psyche. Jerry and his sensibilities were undoubtedly around there as well, soaking up the same vibes. Unbeknownst to him, he would become my destined guru of literature and progenitor to my further developing creative impulses.

I remember the Del Mar Theatre as a major backdrop and repository of Santa Cruz memories of my youth. It was my hangout spot in the seventies and I was hired as an employee there when I turned 16. I consider that illustrious movie theatre lobby as the symbolic corridor to my creative self. Although Santa Cruz has its Boardwalk, the Del Mar Theatre would be my Coney Island of the Mind. In fact, in 2014 I brought Lawrence Ferlinghetti to appear at "Lawrence Ferlinghetti Day" in Santa Cruz at the Del Mar Theatre, hosting the event under my Sparring With Beatnik Ghosts Poetry series umbrella. The scenery of my past, present and future life is projected from that Santa Cruz theatre.

My recollections play out like a movie. Every time I drive northbound on Highway 17, I look west toward Scotts Valley Drive where the Lost World dinosaurs once stood among mounds of development dirt. I wonder if Jerry was digging those behemoths like I was in the late 70s, traveling along with his crackling radio belting out "Dreams" and pot smoke from his VW van, the "harbinger of all old vehicles, forerunner and precursor of our own sad fates," as Kamstra described his van as one of the last holdouts of the artist.

Heading another mile or so down memory lane on highway 17 and further back into Jerry's time machine, I exit Granite Creek Road and imagine the ghostly reappearance of "The Barn" that stood until the '89 quake. To local authorities, The Barn was an unappreciated bohemian haunt, active during the late 1960s, hosting music and counter-culture gatherings. It's walls were festooned with kaleidoscopic light shows, featuring small bands and artists that grew big. Yes, Jerry was there, of course. In addition to being a marijuana smuggler, fisherman, construction worker, artist and writer, Kamstra worked as a club manager for Big Brother & The Holding Company. He hung out with Janis Joplin and other blossoming music stars there. The Barn was like a counter-culture filling station between San Francisco and Big Sur — other stomping grounds of Kamstra on the flower power timeline. The music and goings on of The Barn vanished long before the quake or the sale of dinosaurs or the fall of the Cooper House or the ashes of Positively Front Street and well before the move of Catalyst into the bowling alley on Pacific Garden Mall, the end of KFAT radio or demise of Logos Books.

The footprints of my Generation X in Santa Cruz traversed spots on the map like the two incarnations of the Café Pergolesi, the original Westside Video, Anubis Warpus, the old Atlantis Fantasy World in it's "Lost Boys" location on South Pacific Avenue, and also the dearly-departed, beloved Logos Books and records. That was where my friend and I were first busted with a marijuana joint, sitting on our skateboards in the parking lot behind the bookstore. However, I was feeding my noggin with more tales of fantasy, imagination and poetry at that time than with THC. I was also a young journalist writing for Good Times — which is a definitive crossroads for Jerry Kamstra and me, since Jerry also wrote for the paper and our names shared the masthead from '91 to '95. I was a teen when I started writing at Good Times and always enjoyed Kamstra's cover stories of local flavor and perceived him as a Beatnik Mark Twain. In particular, I remember an article he wrote about the Santa Cruz Flea Market entitled "The Flea and Me" which struck a chord with me because I grew up going to the Flea almost every weekend with my father and formulated a lifelong affinity for the experience.

Even though Jerry and I both wrote for the Good Times at the same time, we wouldn't meet until many years later at the Santa Cruz Flea Market when I was 38 years old. Jerry was selling artwork and books from his trusty VW van and we spoke of art, poetry and literature for three hours, quickly becoming comrades. I invited him to be the headline performer at my next Sparring With Beatnik Ghosts Poetry Reading at the Felix Kulpa Gallery in Santa Cruz.

By the time my journalistic career began as a teen, Kamstra had already written articles, reviews and feature stories for numerous periodicals, including San Francisco Chronicle, San Francisco Bay Guardian, San Francisco Examiner, High Times, Scanlan's Monthly, Beatitude magazine and Desperado. Kamstra's first published article was a homage to Beat novelist Jack Kerouac upon his death which appeared in the San Francisco Sunday Examiner & Chronicle in October, 1969, followed up with an article in the same publication November 16, 1969 titled "Jack's 'Road' was the Beat Children's Beacon." That same year, Kamstra went to Taos, New Mexico to interview actor, producer and director Dennis Hopper, who had just made the film *Easy Rider*, for an article assignment for Scanlan's Monthly, published by Warren Hinckle, political muckraker of the Gonzo journalism genre.

Hinckle's controversial magazine quickly brought heat from the FBI for lambasting the Nixon administration, so some of Kamstra's articles were published under the pseudonym Roger Tichbourne to evade possible federal prosecution of the author for marijuana smuggling.

During his time as a marijuana smuggler from 1966 to 1972, Kamstra sold his story of "Gringo Smugglers" first to Life magazine, who paid him a large advance on the story but refused to publish it once they realized he was the actual gringo smuggler documented in the story. Then Look magazine bought the article, yet reconsidered publishing it because it was too hot for their readership.

An article published in Scanlan's Monthly led to Kamstra's novel *Weed: Adventures of a Dope Smuggler* (Harper & Row, hardback edition, 1974 and Bantam Books paperback edition, 1975). The novel has been optioned by Hollywood producers five times in attempts to make a movie. The first option was from producer Tim Zinnemann in 1974 — intended to star actor Richard Gere in the lead role. Weed sold over 200,000 copies between the Bantam Books and Harper & Row editions combined.

The success of Weed paved the way for the publishing of his novel *The Frisco Kid* (Harper and Row, 1975), heralded as the "San Francisco novel of the year" by Chronicle critic William Hogan upon its release. Famous columnist Herb Caen called it "Intensely readable…a picaresque, Saroyanesque celebration of life in the North Beach netherworld." Kamstra's friend, poet Lawrence Ferlinghetti, owned a cabin in Big Sur, California where Kamstra wrote most of The Frisco Kid. The cabin was also a renowned retreat for other famous authors, most notably Jack Kerouac. The Frisco Kid has become a cult classic which literary critic and Kerouac biographer Gerald Nicosia claims is "a Beat masterpiece on par with On The Road."

This year, I've published the 45th Anniversary Edition of *Weed: Adventures of A Dope Smuggler* and I'm in the process of publishing a Special Edition of *The Frisco Kid*. Both books are published under the Peer Amid Press imprint that Jerry Kamstra started in the seventies. I've inherited the helm from him as publisher of Peer Amid Press.

I would describe Jerry Kamstra as one of my greatest influences on my creative life and like a father, I'm proud to have followed in his footsteps as a community organizer. Kamstra organized literary events from San Francisco to Big Sur, California, including the popular Santa Cruz Poetry Festivals. There were five festivals at the Santa Cruz Civic Auditorium, spanning from 1972 to 1981, which were the largest poetry festivals in the United States. Kamstra was involved with all five of these festivals, and was director of two of them — the 2nd Santa Cruz Poetry Festival "Benefit for AIM-J" (Americans In Mexican Jails) in 1974 and the "Fifth Annual Poet Tree Festive All" in 1981.

Kamstra started the AIM-J organization, and 30 American prisoners in one of Mexico's most notorious prisons received some "getting by" money as a direct result of the AIM-J poetry benefit held in Santa Cruz November 25, 1974. "The reading itself was one of the more exciting events to hit Santa Cruz since the invasion scares of World War II," said Sam Silver of the Berkeley Barb, referring to the bomb scare that took place at the Santa Cruz Civic Auditorium while Allen Ginsberg recited his poetry to a crowd of 1,600 people. Also performing at the '74 festival were Charles Bukowski, Lawrence Ferlinghetti, jazz musician Charles Lloyd and a full-slate of "the biggest names in verse" according to Silver.

The "Fifth Annual Poet Tree Festive All" of November 13-14, 1981 was a two-day event that showcased Lawrence Ferlinghetti, Amiri Baraka, Gregory Corso, Bob Kaufman,

Wanda Coleman, Diane Di Prima, Lorna Dee Cervantes, William Everson and many other performers. Kamstra opened the festival reading Henry Miller to the musical accompaniment of Max Hartstein's 25th Century Ensemble.

Three decades later, Jerry took me under his wing and imparted his knowledge and a lineage of creative energy that prompted me to bring the poetry festival back to Santa Cruz at the Cocoanut Grove Ballroom on 2/12/12, produced by Sparring With Beatnik Ghosts (SWBG). Kamstra's artwork and writing was showcased in several of the SWBG Anthologies, including as the featured artist of Volume 1, Number 4. SWBG published The Buzz From The Bees in its Volume 1, Number 3 Anthology, February 2010 — here's an excerpt:

"At Cape Canaveral they sprayed the mosquitoes to make them dead. Yes they did. And they killed the bird it is said, that when it's dead, even God would count the least of its head — and it's dead. Yes, it's dead. The last Dusky Sparrow is dead."

In 2015, SWBG and its umbrella organization The Mystic Boxing Commission created an archive for artwork, books and memorabilia related to the Sparring With Beatnick Ghosts Poetry Series at the Old Sash Mill complex in downtown Santa Cruz. This archive, dedicated to Kamstra, is known as the Jerry Kamstra Sparring Archive. The Kamstra "Sparchive" has since moved from the Sash Mill to Scotts Valley Drive and onward to Los Angeles, where the Kamstra Sparchive and Peer Amid Press are now headquartered in the NoHo Arts District. Events are held at the Sparchive, which continues to honor Jerry Kamstra with communal gatherings in the Santa Cruz tradition, publishing iconic works, and providing an interactive museum for free expression. Kamstra's book's can be found on Lulu.com, Amazon, as well as local bookstores and at www.SparringArtists.com.

Chapter 8: Memories
by Daniel Wenger

The idea of attempting to collect significant memories of the '60s and '70s has brought me to the realization that my memories are not sequential in the least. So, before writing anything about my life in Santa Cruz, how I got here and what it has meant to me, I have had to spend some time ordering my thoughts and associating dates with significant events.

My father was a psychology professor who eventually ended up at UCLA doing research in the physiological aspects of emotions. His work had carried him in the early 1960s to India. He took with him a multi-pen oscillograph (the precursor of the lie detector) to study the yogis. He was funded to study advanced yogis in various states of consciousness. He came home after a two-year research project with much physiological data and fascinating stories about the yogis that he worked with. His scientific work is referenced in the literature of the Transcendental Meditation Organization.

My mother was an accomplished pianist. She never appeared on stage solo but was a highly desired accompanist, sight-reading and playing with feeling any music put in front of her. My primary connection with my mother was via music. I was introduced to the violin as an 11-year-old and played through junior high school. My family played classical music together with my father on cello and my sister on flute. These are the happiest memories of my family life.

My parents gave me many valuable experiences while I was a child, including classical music concerts, ballets and operas. When I was 16, I moved to Paris with my family for a year and a half while my father was on a Fulbright at the Sorbonne. We traveled around France as well as to England, Spain,

Italy, Germany, Switzerland, Austria, Denmark, Norway and Sweden. In Paris I read some of Sartre, Camus, Nin and Henry Miller, which exposed me to truthful self-examination. It was difficult to reenter the U.S. as an 18-year-old and feel connected to the culture of my peers in Los Angeles.

I met my first wife Anne on the boat returning to the U.S. from France. She was a young intellectual French woman, eight years older than me, coming to the states to study literature. She later became a professor of literature in France and a respected literary critic. I was too young and not well prepared for the experience of marriage. We had one son, Eric, who was born when I was 19. He went with his mother to Paris when he was 9 and I suffered from this separation. As an adult he returned to Los Angeles and we shared a close connection. He died of AIDS in 1984. Anne and I were both with him.

My second wife Clare was, and still is, a Welsh woman who I met in Los Angeles. We had three boys together in the '60s. Our marriage ended and she took the boys back to Wales to raise them. Clare completed a PhD in anthropology and became a professor in Wales. The pain of the separation from my sons is always with me. Two of my sons, Alex and Max, live in Wales, and Matthew, with whom I visit whenever I can, lives in Seattle..

After receiving my PhD in theoretical physics in 1967 and teaching physics for a year and a half, I found myself not liking teaching and having no connection with physics research. After two failed marriages and the loss of contact with my four children, I was not enjoying life.

In the early spring of 1969 I went through a several day process of deep recognition that my current life was not worth living. But, there was something that I realized that I did enjoy doing, and could do instead of leaving this world, and that was working with my hands. I remembered the hobby room of my childhood.

The hobby room was an unfinished room in the home that my parents built in 1946 when we came to Los Angeles. My father and I finished the interior of the room and created a workshop with tools and a dark room. I spent hours in this room next to the fireplace working with my hands. In 1969 a fundamental change occurred in me. I felt that there was a new life ahead for me. The excitement that I felt was vivid and enduring.

During the previous year, while teaching physics during the week, I would teach gliding on the weekends in fixed wing gliders to students who would come to Crystalaire Airport in the Mojave desert. I had learned to fly and earned my instructor rating in 1968 and spent my weekends in Sweitzer gliders soaring over the mountains and desert. I slept in my bus and enjoyed the quiet and dark nights. One of my students, David Scott, was a sandal maker in Hollywood. He offered to teach me leatherwork and I quickly learned to make sandals for my friends and myself. I loved the beauty of latigo leather. I decided that making sandals would be my new direction in life. I would work with leather, meet new people and make sandals for them.

Not long after that decision, I moved to a simple cabin in lower Topanga Canyon outside of Los Angeles. The location has been called the Snake Pit, but to me it was heaven, next to a creek with no view of neighbors, and frogs singing all night long. My cabin was covered in a form of bamboo that grew locally. It was just a few hundred yards up the creek from the beach and I learned to run the path along the creek in the dark. I set up my workspace outside of the cabin and did all my sandal making there. It was also where I made my original Lotus chair using latigo leather and steel.

I still to this day prefer to work outside when possible. The beach and the friends who lived there were my treasures. Life had a new flavor. No schedule, no clear vision of the future, but a vivid appreciation of the present and the joy of crafting something useful and beautiful. These were the years of abundant chemical exploration and I did inhale and experiment and enjoy.

In the summer of 1969 I took to my red and beige 1960 Westfalia VW camper for travels along the California coast to explore new places where people were also experiencing their own new directions in life. I took a tea chest of a favorite smoky lapsang souchong tea that had a very special ability to calm one down and produce a very peaceful state. I stopped at every new-age grocery store that I could find and sang the merits of my tea and traded it for food. On return trips to the same market I would be greeted with enthusiasm and requests for more tea. I packaged the tea in baggies with my own label, "Tai Ping Tea," and was very comfortable in my nomadic life.

I stopped in Santa Cruz area to visit Joan Felt, an acquaintance from Los Angeles who had moved to Brookdale. Joan was living in a dormitory and was happy to see me. She introduced me to the Oganookie band and I became friends with the entire group. In fact, after I settled in the area I became a groupie, catching every concert of theirs at the Catalyst and the Town & County in Ben Lomond and even once following them to the Bay Area for another chance to dance to their "Black Jack Davey."

I returned to my Topanga cabin and made more versions of my Lotus chair, which was originally inspired by the Katavolos T-Chair that had been in my parents' home in Los Angeles. That chair was very attractive but not comfortable. I had set out to make a chair in leather and steel that was attractive and comfortable as well. From the attention that the chair was getting, I realized that I had designed something that people enjoyed.

I was interested in moving out of the Los Angeles area, so I packed my chair making tools and other belongings into my bus and headed north with no idea of where I would land. With my arc welder and oxy-acetylene tanks just in the back and a new life ahead of me, I explored the little towns along Highway 1 and 101.

While passing through Santa Cruz, I shopped to pick up a lovely young woman who was hitchhiking at the corner of River Street and Highway 1 (the intersection was more hospitable to hitching a ride at that time). Julie Zoll needed a ride to her home in Aptos and I was happy to oblige. She showed me her home and her bed swinging from four ropes attached to the ceiling. When I left Aptos, headed to Topanga, I realized that if I were to set up a workshop in Santa Cruz I would have a friend in Julie, as well as Joan in Brookdale.

Soon I reconnected with Julie, who took me to the new General Feed and Hardware. The place was in an old barn on the deserted property of the Pacific Lumber Company on Soquel Drive just west of 41st. Next to the barn was a workshop with two wooden-boat builders (one or both later moved to Port Townsend in Washington). This was a sweet spot with potential for a space for me and my tools. I was told by Bruce Bratton at the barn to contact Mr. Rittenhouse in downtown Santa Cruz. Mr. Rittenhouse proved to be a friendly and accepting person who told me about the old "coffee room" of the lumberyard, a 20' x 20' x 20' space on the road behind General Feed and Hardware. The space had a door and window facing west to the access road and a double garage-door back wall that lifted and exposed the entire space to the air and to another access road of the lumberyard. For $50 a month I did not hesitate to take the space as my home

Daniel Wenger

and shop.

In one corner of the coffee room was a small office-like space with a loft overhead. The loft became my sleeping quarters. I bought a refrigerator, a small electric stove, and with the existing sink and running cold water, I had a home. I was in this space for the next four years, from early summer 1970 until sometime in 1974 when I moved my workshop to the Old Sash Mill off River Street in Santa Cruz.

I loved my coffee room studio and the rhythm of my daily life. I would wake up with ideas for new designs, go out for breakfast at a place on Seabright just south of Murray St., return to the shop and work all day till dark, then drive to the Catalyst for a bite to eat and a beer and to dance to the music. The Catalyst was my evening living room.

My shop became a draw for others to visit. The door was always open, never locked, and I would often come home to find guests or bring friends with me. My cast iron stove, recovered from an old mushroom farm at the northern end of Swanton Road, had a tall stack going 20 feet up to the ceiling. I would have two or three or four Lotus chairs in front of the fire (the fire made at different times with wood, coal or oil) and enjoy life with friends or alone. I had a neighbor who lived across Soquel Drive who would make a batch of chili and bring me enough to fuel me for days on end.

I had met Ramblin' Jack Elliott at a beach party in Malibu and whenever he came to town to see his daughter Aiyana he would visit me in Soquel. Jack would talk and talk and I would listen and listen, and I cherish those memories so much. We traveled to Los Angeles together with Jack playing his guitar in the seat next to me. Jack's music was wonderful to hear wherever he played.

Charles Lloyd was another friend from my Topanga days. I had made him a director's chair that is his favorite chair to this day. The saxophone case that I made for him was frankly fantastic, made with yellow latigo leather and a sheepskin lining. It is too bad that it was left, along with his beautiful instrument, in a taxi in New York, never to be seen again. Where is it now? Charles would come to Santa Cruz to play at the Catalyst and other spots in the area. One memorable night, while listening to him transition from chaos to serenity on the stage of the Catalyst, I came to some understanding of the power of jazz and his music.

Peter Troxel, the manager of Oganookie, and I became friends. Peter would take beautiful photos of the furniture that I designed and made, photos that I still use today to show my work.

Bill Burke, a physicist, would come by and we would share time together. This was my only connection with my past as a physicist.

During the latter part of those four years in Soquel I also rented a cabin on East Cliff Drive near Moran Lake. This cabin had some property around it and had been used by a candle maker who moved to Australia. I jumped at the chance to rent it and enjoyed a bit more comfort than I had in my studio in Soquel. This cabin became the birthing home for Julie's daughter Marigold and for my friend Jan Arnold's daughter Ami. Neither were my children but the cabin had the right vibes for these two ladies. Kate Bowland was midwife for Marigold and I was midwife (midhusband) for Ami.

One day the owners wanted to sell the cabin and offered it to me with the land for $40,000. I did not have $40,000 and did not have the mindset to ask to borrow it, so this wonderful property passed on to others. In 2010 the land was sold for $5,000,000.

In 1973 Kohoutek, a new comet, appeared in the sky. The local astronomers had published the celestial position of the comet but that did not tell me where to look in the sky. I decided that what I needed was a celestial globe with a terrestrial globe just inside it. I set myself to making this device and after three prototypes, I came up with my UniGlobe. The measuring devices on the UniGlobe allowed me to know where in the sky to find the comet, and one night I did see it. Very satisfying.

I used the UniGlobe to teach celestial navigation on the beach next to the Crow's Nest. The class would "shoot the sun" with a sextant and then go into O'Neill's and work the calculations with the assistance of the device that I had made.

While playing with the UniGlobe I realized that it could be used as a sundial. It was from the UniGlobe that I was able to design and fabricate a unique and educational device for telling the time by the sun and determining the time of sunrise and sunset. Grace Slick's father, who was a patent attorney, lived a few houses down the road on East Cliff. He worked with me to receive a patent and thus the recognition of the originality of my sundial. In 1977 I received a grant from the County Arts Program to place a sundial in San Lorenzo Park in Santa Cruz. Alas, it proved to be too much of an attraction for vandals with slingshots, and after replacing it three times I gave up. Another sundial was installed behind the Lawrence Hall of Science in Berkeley. Sadly, it too was vandalized and removed. Today over 35 sundials exist in private collections in Europe, Mexico, Chile and the U.S. I still make a dial from time to time.

Soon after moving into my studio in Soquel I was able to explore an idea that developed while making constructions for an artist friend. I realized that if I cut a corner off a cube and then let the exposed surface become the floor of the object, I end up with a structure with three square pitched roofs and a hexagonal floor space. In 1970, soon after moving into my

Soquel studio I constructed a skeletal version of this space using 4x4 redwood beams and plywood gussets. I found that I could hang three hammocks from the three mid points of the structure and thereby create a very nice communal environment. A hammock cube was placed in front of Pan's Restaurant at the Sash Mill and was often filled to capacity with three people in each hammock.

    I moved completely out of my Soquel studio and into the Sash Mill in about 1975. This allowed me access to woodworking tools at SunSeeker Wood Creations and space for a new metal shop next door, and for a clean room where I could draw and display my chairs. After giving up my Soquel studio and my East Cliff cabin, I relied again on my VW bus as a home. At that time the Sash Mill was a beehive of creativity and Pan's Restaurant a center for socializing.

    SunSeeker had been started by Jim Grodzins. Jim had invited other woodworkers to share in the space, including Tom Nedelsky, Karl Bareis and Jim Miller. Jim invited me to set up a workspace among the wood working tools in exchange for teaching him trigonometry.

    From my work in theoretical physics I had explored some math problems that still held my interest. I had started work on a random walk problem that I thought I could solve. Work on this problem proceeded on and off for over 10 years and ultimately led me to a simple, elegant solution, what mathematicians call a closed-form solution to a non-trivial problem.

    One day at the Sash Mill a friend of Jim's, the dancer Nita Little, came to visit with her friend Annica Rose. The two had been traveling together and were visiting Santa Cruz. By that evening Annica and I had established a connection that exists to this day. Annica and I had both experienced the loss of our children and were wanting the joys of family. It was not long before our son Sam was on his way. My experiences with two births in my East Cliff cabin prepared me for Sam's birth in 1977. I was again midwife (midhusband) for Annica's birthing of Sam.

Although Annica and I are still close we have followed our own paths, Annica with two more sons and a life bringing yoga to people of restricted mobility and to children in school. Her Adaptive Yoga Project lives on with the support of those that Annica has trained. On my side I was so lucky to meet Katherine McCleary, my current wife and partner for life. Thank you Raven Lang for bringing Katherine and me together.

About 1979, needing more income to raise Sam, I gave up chair making and returned to using skills I had acquired prior to entering the graduate school in physics at UCLA. In 1957 I had taken my first post-college job, a computer programming position in the U.S. Space Program. Working at Ramo Wooldridge and later the Space Technology Laboratory gave me a good experience with computing in the early years of that field. By 1980 I had returned to computing, doing consulting work from my small trailer in an apple orchard at the Trout Gulch Co-op School. I lived on the property and Sam went to school with children ranging from three to 14 years old. Elsa Etcheverry was the glue that kept that school together and I have wonderful memories of that time, including the exciting flood of 1982 when we spent the night in the loft of the barn on the school grounds.

In 1983 I moved my trailer to Bonny Doon and lived there for 10 years. Sam lived part-time with me and part-time with Annica. In 1985 I took a job at UCSC as Computing Director for the Humanities Division. I retired in 1999 and took up rock-climbing, a passion that I still enjoy today. I began making chairs again in 2009 after Los Angeles-based gallery owners Scott and Joanna Nadeau tracked me down and asked me to return to making chairs. It turns out that, unknown to me at the time, there was a demand for my pieces from the '70s. Sam joined me in 2013 making chairs and we have built a studio together in the garage of my home with Katherine.

Santa Cruz has been a rich and rewarding place to live my life. I am so grateful for all of the events that brought me to this wonderful spot on the globe.

Chapter 9: Tom Noddy, the Bubble Man
by Tom Noddy

Going south to head east, but just after passing Junipero Serra with his giant finger pointing west, old Van Dorf's radiator blew steam. I took the advice of the big Catholic statue and turned toward the cooling coastal fog. Leaving Hwy 280 on to 92, Van Dorf bubbled and boiled and I knew we wouldn't be climbing the Sierras or skirting the Mojave; the trip to New Mexico was off. Compression was down; once we were up to the top of the hill we mostly coasted down to Half-Moon Bay.

We were broken down, but my Van Dorf could probably handle the smaller ups and downs of Hwy 1 for a while, we didn't have to be broken down in Half Moon Bay. The map showed the next bay to the south held a town called Santa Cruz. I once met a couple of street jugglers from Santa Cruz who called themselves the Flying Karamazov Brothers. Yeah, let's go be broken down in Santa Cruz!

That was 1977 and I'm still here, not quite broken down but … still here.

I'd built a puppet stage into the curbside window of that big Ford van, along with the bed, cupboards and sink. The plan was to pull up to parks and empty lots and present weekend shows while looking to see if the college campus and whatever clubs and bars might make room for my shows: Tom Noddy and the Travelin' Puppets, Political, Social & Spiritual Satire. I also had some bubble tricks that I performed, but for the many outdoor shows, even a little bit of wind would make that impossible.

I became a street performer downtown, played the breaks for musicians in the clubs, organized variety shows and after my Bubble Magic performance was featured on Johnny

Carson's Tonight Show (1983 twice and 1984) and David Letterman's Late Show (2007) I took gigs across the country and around the world but I never left Santa Cruz

Santa Cruz Ordinance 9.50.020 Conduct on Public Property, Monuments, and Lawns, says: "No person, after having been notified by a law enforcement officer that he or she is in violation of the prohibition in this section, shall:.. (d) In the…CBD central business districts, intentionally throw, discharge launch, or spill any solid object (including but not limited to footballs, hacky sacks, baseballs, beach balls, Frisbees, or other similar devices) or liquid substances (with the exception of bubble street performers who otherwise comply with all applicable statutes and ordinances) or otherwise cause any object or substance to be thrown, discharged, launched, spilled, or to become airborne."

Okay, the City Council of Santa Cruz, California didn't actually intend to outlaw juggling when they passed their set of new "downtown ordinances" in the summer of 2002. They actually meant to send the Hacky Sack players packing.

The downtown sidewalks have never been a perfect location for street performing — there are only a few places where a large crowd might gather — but that didn't keep the Flying Karamazov Brothers from starting out there. Tom Noddy launched his career by performing Bubble Magic along with his puppet show there, Bob Brozman, Thoth, Gillian Welch, and others have graced this coastal community with their skills over the years. But in 2002, the "progressive" City Council, responding to a fevered campaign set off by the downtown merchants and the local daily newspaper, which offered up the performers as scapegoats for the decline in business income downtown. They didn't seem to notice that the entire country, and the world, were in the midst of a decline in retail sales.

To be fair, most of the proffered "downtown ordinances" were really meant to regulate or restrict panhandling or generally sitting around. But the special efforts that had always been made to exempt street performers from these kinds of laws were now set aside in a hurried effort to get some new laws on the books before the Council went into summer break. And there was this one special Hacky Sack ordinance.

The legitimate concern was that sports activity on the downtown sidewalk by groups of young men intent on their game sometimes endangered other passersby (or "low income seniors" as the local newspaper explained it to those who may not have understood the urgency).

But then, why stop at Hacky Sack if they are going to go to all the trouble to pass a law? They lifted some wordage from some other city's ordinance and it seemed to cover other antisocial behavior as well. ("Liquid substance"? Spitting maybe?) They did then worry that this would set them up for ridicule. Was it possible that some police officer in the future might use this law to stop bubble blowing? In the town that is the home of the world's first professional bubble blower? Tom Noddy had gone from performing on the sidewalks of Santa Cruz directly to three appearances on the Tonight Show back in the 1980s. Now he travels the world presenting his Bubble Magic to audiences in nightclubs, universities, theaters, mathematics conferences and other venues. (He also sometimes finds himself writing about himself in the third person.).

They added this peculiar bubble-blower's exemption to the city's municipal code "...with the exception of bubble street performers who otherwise comply with all applicable statutes and ordinances." My friends teased me about my "political pull" when they saw that, but when Tim Furst of the Karamazovs pointed out to me that the wording of the proposed law could allow it to be used to stop jugglers I was much less amused by the special exemption for bubbles.

    I came back to town and met with City Council members just before they did the "second reading" of the proposal. A majority vote on this reading would make it a new law to be enforced downtown. I told the Council members that it could outlaw juggling and they assured me that it would not. They thought that I was just putting the worst face on what they were doing. They knew that I also opposed their other proposals that would force all street performers to step away from the buildings and only perform at the curbside, facing inward. But this anti-juggling addition was of another order and I just couldn't get them to sit down and look at it reasonably. It clearly would outlaw juggling and they insisted that it wouldn't. They were on a fast moving train and they wouldn't slow down and look around. I asked one of them if, before voting, he wouldn't, at least, ask the City Attorney at the Council meeting if this wouldn't outlaw juggling downtown and when he did, the City Attorney leaned forward to the microphone and simply said "No." They passed the law while assuring me that it would not outlaw juggling.

    One year later, I was walking down Pacific Avenue and saw a police officer interrupting the performance of a young clown. He was delighting a crowd that included over a dozen cherubic children. I overheard the officer explaining to the clown that juggling was now illegal in Santa Cruz.

    Sigh!.

    No sense arguing with the cop; she was reading the text of the law the same way that I had read it last year. I went back to the City Council and met with several of them individually. Some thought that they remembered that juggling might have been excluded from this law; others didn't remember anything of the sort. In either case, it was plain from the reading of the text that juggling was outlawed: it IS, they now assured me, the law in Santa Cruz that one cannot juggle downtown. When I asked if they intended to change that law they explained that that's a very complicated matter.

So I rummaged through my toy box and found some balls, and also found some old Karamazov clubs in my collection. I printed copies of the law, picked up some lemons, and called the press to announce that at 2:00pm the next day I would be juggling in "apparent violation" of the law downtown in front of the police/downtown hosts substation in the old Delmarette building.

Let me confess here. I'm an excellent bubble blower, maybe the best. (That isn't much of a brag; remember, every bubble that I've ever blown has popped.) But I ain't much of a juggler. My friend Tim Furst had agreed to come down from Seattle to juggle if it was needed to make a point. However, the moment had arrived and Tim was far away. The law didn't specify that only good juggling was illegal; bad jugglers qualified as outlaws too, and I felt fully qualified.

The news cameras rolled, the print media interviewed me, and friends gathered, but no police showed up in front of the Delmarette. The press left and my friends wandered off (a reflection perhaps on my ability to hold a crowd with my juggling skills). I juggled balls, I juggled lemons, I tried to juggle those big ol' clubs, I even crumpled up copies of the law and juggled those. No cops; no ticket.

I did want to get the ticket. I was in town, I knew the law, I knew the history of the passage of the law, I was a known character in town, I could speak to the issue better than most, and I wanted the test case to be soon, before they chased other jugglers from town like they had with that young clown. I picked up my props and went down the street and found a willing police officer. She was polite, her supervisor was polite, I juggled three lemons, and they cited me. I didn't want to sign the citation and have the case fade away when I went to court and the police stayed away; I wanted attention on this case and the press was gone now, so I declined to sign the citation. That meant that they'd take me in front of a judge and I could talk to a judge and then to jail.

This is normally a "book and release" situation. A quick photo and fingerprinting (who knows, I may be an international juggling outlaw wanted by the feds or Interpol) and then let me go. Usually it takes an hour, two if they are very busy. In my case it took 13 hours. They kept me in the holding tank while drunks came in, sobered up, and were released. At 6 a.m. the next day I was released. I went home and wrote about my experience for the press, the City Council members, and for some juggler friends. I sent out the email and within a day the same email list received letters from the Flying Karamazov Brothers announcing that they would come home to Santa Cruz to juggle downtown. The Ks are adored here in town — "Loco Boys Make Good on Broadway/Hollywood/Internationally": stories are written whenever they move their art to the next level.

The city of Santa Cruz passed the law on June 24, 2002. On June 26, 2003, I was arrested for juggling. For one year juggling was outlawed in this town. On June 27, the day after my arrest, the Karamazovs and others suggested that they and other jugglers would come to town to violate that unjust law.

I imagined City Council members trembling as they read the letters that told of the K's intent to put out a call to jugglers at the International Jugglers' Association convention to come to town to join us for some illegal juggling fun. I booked a hall to accommodate a nighttime show/demonstration to follow the day of juggle arrests. Political work just got to be really fun.

Thirteen days later, on July 9, 2003, the Santa Cruz City Council passed an "emergency resolution" to re-legalize juggling.

Santa Cruz, July 24, 2002

"Ordinance 9.50.020 Conduct on Public Property, Monuments, and Lawns:

(e) Notwithstanding subsections (d), individual bubble street performers and individual jugglers who otherwise comply with all applicable statutes and ordinances are authorized to blow bubbles and juggle."

I do love that, in the midst of war abroad, homeland security crises in America, and budget crises here in town, the matter of juggling had risen to the state of "emergency."

Chapter 10: I Can Do This Work!
My Journey into Midwifery
by Karen Ehrlich

The day I was born, in October 1946, my mother went to her regular prenatal visit with her doctor. It was two weeks before my due date and my father was out of town, taking my two older brothers to stay with an aunt for my mother's tenderest weeks. When the doctor examined my mother, he told her that she was about to have her baby and to go directly to the hospital.

I was my mother's third child. She had sensed no signs that she was about to give birth, and argued with the doctor. But he insisted that she go to the hospital without delay. She went, but spent the afternoon pacing the floors, furious, and smoking many cigarettes. When he arrived in the evening, my mother began to state her case: "I know when I'm in labor. I'm not in labor. It is ridiculous for me to be here. I've had two babies, and I know when I'm in labor."

He responded that he'd check her and let her go home if there were no changes. She climbed onto the bed, opened up her legs, and there I was — about to emerge.

Some years ago, I was sitting in my house in the evening, rocking in front of the fire. l had been up all the previous night at a birth, and had come home and slept for a while. Now I was drifting in a dark, warm fog. I began to feel myself in utero, sensing the need to be released into my own life. My mother was not ready for me to arrive and was not registering my messages. I knew I needed to be born that day and had to make my entrance by the strength of my own will. After I came out, my sense of relief and pride that I had prevailed was keenly, strongly powerful. I now relate that entry to my lifelong ways of creating my destiny by the strength of my own will.

As a little girl, I was fascinated with infants. I thought they were the most wonderful creatures ever. For many years my ambition was to be a nurse — in the nursery with tiny babies. When I learned that there was such a thing as birth care, I added maternity nursing to my list of possibilities. However, by the age of eight I had become a theater and acting devotee. That ambition persisted throughout high school, and thoughts of nursing were abandoned.

College was a difficult time for me. My parents would not allow me to major in theater, because they thought that such a degree would qualify me to do nothing. My dream derailed, I wanted to take a year or two off from school to figure out what I wanted to study and do. But my parents also refused to allow me to take time away from my education, saying that I would never get a degree if I dropped out. At 17, I didn't have an inkling that I could walk away from their emotional support, so I enrolled in a school I didn't want to attend, in a major I didn't want to study.

During my sophomore year, the Peace Corps recruited on my campus. The recruiter had served for two years in the middle of her undergraduate education and convinced me that I could contribute to our world even at 19 or 20. I applied, full of hope, ideals, and enthusiasm. But most of my references were relatives and family friends who believed that my parents knew what was best for me and recommended that I be accepted only after I had finished college. My application was denied.

I was crushed. My only choice at the time seemed to be continue in college. The end result was two more disconsolate years of college that left me with a powerful aversion toward ever again going to school.

Once I had graduated I was determined to no longer allow

anyone else to tell me how to live my life. I worked at a radio station for a year, but truly didn't know what I wanted to do, so I packed up my car and headed west — intent on turning my world upside down and trusting that I would land on my feet. For six weeks I stopped ·here and there as I drove cross-country, then up to the Pacific Northwest where I thought I'd settle in.

Instead, one day I threw everything back into my car and drove back to the San Francisco Bay Area. There I found an apartment to share, a new best friend, support for my questioning of everything I'd grown up with, and a counter culture that was fascinatingly alive with new promise. Freedom of movement and expression were captivating.

People were taking their lives into their own hands and doing what they knew was right for them. Everywhere around me people were questioning authority and institutions, refusing to accept arbitrary and artificial restrictions and boundaries. Outrageousness was in. The year was 1969.

Within a year I met two women who planned to give birth in their own homes. They talked about wanting to be immersed in the experience without their babies' arrivals being turned into something antiseptic, dehumanizing, and institutionalized. They wanted to be free of the potential harm that hospitals could inflict on what they saw as a natural event. It sounded interesting.

The next year found me traveling in Europe. In Holland I visited a family with two young children who had been born at home, amidst celebration and friends. My hostess liked it that way. She couldn't see any reason to put childbirth into a setting of illness.

Then I spent a year in England. My first week there I met a woman who was newly pregnant. Our lives became intertwined. While Britain's tradition of birth at home had persisted into the 1970s, she was required to have her baby in a hospital. A big push was on in England to get women out of their homes for birth via a growing list of contraindications: having a first baby, higher than a second-floor walkup, no hot running water, no inside toilet. In 1972 when she gave birth, about 84% of British women were already having their babies in hospitals.

Later in that year I also met a woman who had recently given birth to her fifth child. She had almost died from a problem that had arisen, and her doctor had told her that she had to stop having babies. This was distressing to her: she loved being pregnant, giving birth, and nursing infants. Perhaps, she mused to me, as second best she would go into midwifery training.

When she mentioned becoming a midwife, a light bulb lit up in my brain — kindling a memory of something I had long ago pondered and long since forgotten. I asked her, "How do you become a midwife?"

She described several years of schooling. Immediately I discarded the idea. If it meant going back to school, I wasn't going to have anything to do with it.

After returning home to California, I began to hear more and more about homebirth. Women were taking their power into their own hands and giving birth where, how and with whom they chose — most frequently with midwives, a professional class that had been nearly wiped out throughout North America. Now, newly minted renegade midwives were teaching themselves and each other how to attend a woman in labor.

A tantalizing aura of outlaw came along with midwifery. The profession had been suppressed in the US and Canada from the late 1800s onward and mostly eliminated by the middle of the 1900s. Now, in the face of the 1970s counterculture, the nonconformists with whom I lived were creating a renaissance of this ancient calling. Strongly opposed by the medical powers-that-be, midwifery had to grow in the underground. Everything about this movement, this reawakening, appealed to me, despite potential legal risks. My fantasies of entering' the field grew daily.

But I also hesitated. I had finished college more than five years before and had done nothing that even faintly resembled schooling since. My aversion to college still loomed large. Would I manage to stick with this new interest long enough to actually become a midwife?

Because I wasn't ready to let anyone know about this dream, in case I didn't finish what I had begun, I started to read about childbirth on my own, on the sly, in secret. Everything I read fascinated me. Every bit of knowledge left me wanting to know more. I slowly owned up to this yearning with my closest friends, who encouraged me. Remarkably, in my free time after work, I found myself studying. For the first time in 10 years, learning was fun.

I heard about a beginners' midwife study group in my area. I sought it out and joined. I worked at San Francisco State University at the time. A one-semester class entitled "Pregnancy, Childbirth, and the Newborn" was being offered by the Nursing Department and was scheduled during the noon hour. I audited it for three semesters, refusing to enroll officially and be forced to study, write papers, take exams. My essential knowledge base crystallized.

During the first semester, I met a woman who was a part of the San Francisco Women's Health Collective. That organization was about to hire a midwife couple to teach a course about birth. Then the collective would present an ongoing series of alternative pregnancy and childbirth workshops. Was I interested? I signed up.

The International Childbirth Education Association had a chapter in Marin County, where I lived. Among their upcoming plans was to launch a training program for volunteer labor coaches who would then be available to accompany women as advocates and guides. I enrolled.

I worked and studied for 1-1/2 years before I had the chance to attend my first labor. Following two days of pain, lack of progress, psychosocial turmoil, and emotional anguish, the mother was transported to a hospital for an epidural. I was then excluded from the delivery room for her forceps birth. Having been awake with her for two solid nights, when I found my exhausted way to my bed, I collapsed into oblivion as soon as my head hit my pillow. As I awoke and climbed back into consciousness, I heard my inner voice say, *I can do this work!* Despite the agony that I had seen, heard, and felt, I came away more committed than ever.

A friend and former housemate of mine asked me to help at her birth. After a long, failure-to-progress labor that led to possible fetal distress, she had a cesarean. The energy of helping her was riveting.

Another good friend had moved from the Bay Area and was having her second baby with the Santa Cruz Birth Center. I was her companion throughout labor and her wonderful, healthy birth. This thoroughly confirmed my path. I did my first vaginal exams and was correct in my assessments. The midwife liked my energy and encouraged me to apply for an apprenticeship with the birth center collective, then offered to apprentice me herself. I made plans to move to Santa Cruz.

Another friend was a childbirth educator. A student in her class was going to give birth at home and asked my friend to midwife her. My friend then asked me to assist. The birth was delightful. After the baby was born, this first-time midwife began to shake with exhilaration and nerves and asked me to deliver the placenta.

I was hooked. Midwifery had everything I felt I needed. It was poetry and science, spirit and politics, simplicity and complexity, woman-powered and man-in-volved, defying institutions and hooked into advances in knowledge. It entailed service and responsibility, humility and leadership, common sense, and rock solid knowledge.

My apprenticeship was thin. By the time I got to town, the Santa Cruz Birth Center had disbanded its collective and my mentor was burned out and winding down her practice. After I had worked with her for only eight births, she went off call. She graduated me, telling me that she thought I was ready to go out on my own. I was dumbfounded and more than hesitant. She suggested that I partner with another new midwife so that we could support each other and fill in where the other was weak. For each of the first 10 births we worked together, we called someone to consult over problems, and over the next months we began to feel more grounded.

After I had attended about 35 births, I believed that I knew what I was doing. Then, working as a solo practitioner, after I had attended 50 births, I knew that I was a midwife. Yet within myself I was compelled to get 100 births under my belt. I felt that I needed to have been responsible for that many mothers and babies in order to be credible to the midwifery community and even to myself. I could not ease up until I reached that landmark.

In that process, I wore out utterly. I had no children, nor was I in a relationship. When I heard midwives with families say that they did three or four births a month, I surmised that I should be able to manage five or six. But for me, six births a month proved to be too much, espeeially along with the three or four child birth classes and support groups I taught each week.

I began to do primary care in August of 1976. In May of 1977 I had seven births in seven days; in the next two weeks I delivered five more babies. That was 12 babies in three weeks — not over the two to three month span that my calendar expected. It was an overload I never completely recovered from while actively and more-than-full time attending births. Despite coming back from a vacation in August feeling rested and ready, by October I was seriously overextended. My nervous system and I had gotten a divorce. Not only was I wearing out, but1 had hardly any personal life to replenish myself and no time to develop one.

I cut back on my monthly commitments but, by the time I was actually doing fewer births six months later, I was increasingly bone-weary. I began to cut down on my numbers again, then realized that my residual exhaustion was so great that I simply had to quit. In June, following a particularly hard, long, stressful birth, I decided that, for the foreseeable future, I must take on no more.

Two weeks after I had decided to quit taking on births, my best friend called from southern California with the news that she was pregnant and wanted me to midwife her for a January birth. I wholeheartedly said yes. The next month a sister midwife walked into my office to tell me she was pregnant and ask if I would take care of her. Again I immediately and excitedly agreed, then quickly realized that I was going to have to start saying no even to my closest friends. The next month, while in a sweat lodge with my dearest midwife friend — the one with whom I worked most closely and who knew intimately how burned out I was — I noticed that her breasts and belly were growing. She hadn't told me she had a new baby coming because she knew I was turning down dear friends. I tried to say no, but I was totally unable to stay away. I called her and asked her if I could be her midwife. She cried.

I was winding down, yet I had six more months of important promises already made. In November, with only three more births scheduled, a baby in my care died. She had a congenital anomaly that had not been detected during ultrasounds, which caused a severe buildup of fluids and gases in her abdomen. As she was being born, her swollen belly got jammed so firmly in her mother's pelvis that only her head could spontaneously emerge from her mother's body. Assuming shoulder dystocia, while we furiously struggled to free her, she died in my hands. Mourning the life that was lost, I was in deep grief and totally drained, empty, and frazzled. Yet I had made three more heartfelt commitments to cherished friend — births that I was completely unwilling to miss.

I came to believe that the only way I would be able to refuse any more of my loved ones was to leave the country. I planned a trip to Europe for the month after my last due date. I did not schedule a return flight.

When my friend down south gave birth, everything had been straightforward until the moments of the baby's emergence. When my godson's head was born, his body went no where. This was exactly what the still birth had looked like in November. Instantaneously, I plunged into the desperation I had felt when I had to turn a mother with a stuck baby over to a hostile rescue squad. After going through all the accepted steps to release her, without results, I had been dragging at that dying baby's body.

Now, months later, here I was dragging on my godson's body. Luckily, and within seconds, my sense and training prevailed and I began the step-by-step tricks for resolving stuck shoulders. I asked mom to turn onto her hands and knees. As soon as she began to shift her hips, her little boy easily slid out, angry and protesting. After that, I crumpled, utterly incapable of helping my friend in her postpartum.

The next two of my friends' births, my last before I could fully rest, thankfully and happily went well. Then my partner midwife developed a wretched postpartum infection. She tried to heal herself without Western medications while I nursed her. Finally we both gave up. She took antibiotics and dramatically improved. Shortly after her recovery, I flew away.

For months in the Scottish Highlands, I slept. A lot. I groomed and fed horses and drove a car full of luggage deep into the wilds of Scotland. For months I jumped when the telephone rang, panicked that someone needed me and had managed to find me — even here with the Scottish midsummer sun pouring into northern windows at 11 o'clock at night.

Still, after five months I grew eager to be home. I assumed that I would take up my work again, Then someone asked me what I was going to do about births. Out of the blue I blurted, "I'm not going to do any."

I immediately realized that my outburst was correct. If I was ever going to establish my personal life, give myself space to let love into my days and nights, learn my limits so that I could take strong care of myself, I had to leave other people's beds and lives out of my own.

Despite the unmatched ecstasy and fulfillment I receive when I have given everything that birth demands, by the time I return home I am often at minus zero. Midwifery is a life of meeting many women every month, coming to know them in their deepest selves, coming to love them and their families, being at the beck and call of their timetables and dramas, greeting and adoring their newborns, seeing them through the profound changes of the early postpartum time, and then separating from them and moving on to the next ones approaching birth. Such a life is profoundly rich, intense, and devoted. Such a life is full of adrenalin, fiercely exhausting, and depleting. Birth becomes an imperious teacher, an incomparable and exquisite delight, a formidable and sometimes tormenting challenger, a troublesome taskmistress, an inconvenient and ungovernable friend. She demands everything we are, everything we have — and more.

I never could stay away from birth completely, though. Over the next five years, as a few of my closest friends got pregnant, I was too jealous to allow another midwife to attend them while they completed their families. Helping my closest friends, the ones I already adored, whose relationships with me were already mutual and part of my history and life, those years were some of the most meaningful and rewarding of my midwifery career.

I wondered during those years if I would ever again attend births for strangers. But my friends were getting older and stopped having babies and, as I emerged from those precious years of midwifing my inner circle, I found that I was still emphatically a midwife. So I took on the challenge of figuring out how to attend births in my cominunity-at-large while keeping my nervous system intact. I was intent on figuring out how to continue doing this work.

Fehruary 1988

Addendum-30 years later

I never finished writing this piece when I began it all those years ago. I do not recall exactly what I was planning to write next. And now both I and the world of midwifery have changed and grown.

Over the last 40+ years, many states and provinces have prosecuted midwives. In California from 1974 to 1993 more than 50 midwives were prosecuted for practicing medicine without a license.

Some of the US States and Canadian Provinces have now officially recognized this time-honor discipline. In California, direct entry midwifery became a licensed profession in 1993. Efforts to re-establish and strengthen direct entry midwifery are national and international.

Throughout these years, I have been a part of the political work of restoring midwifery. As those efforts evolved, instead of the bootstrap midwifery that my friends and I revived and recreated, we now have schools for direct entry midwifery.

In 2015 I retired from active midwifery. I continue my commitment to this work by, ironically, becoming part of the structure that authorizes our direct entry schools.

I do not miss the disturbed sleep cycles, the peculiar limbo of being on call, the overarching and relentless focus on other people's lives. I do miss the intensity of the work, the magic of birth, the warm and earnest relationships with growing families. I miss the new born babies.

But birth is big, and the work is hard. I am no longer able to sustain birth's intensity. My psyche no longer thrives on dedication to other people's needs over my own and those of my dear ones. Keeping up with new developments that affect maternal and newborn care became a burdensome irritation. This aging brain and aging body are not as agile as they once were (midwifery can be a contortionist's art). Communication and information, so important to young families and their midwives, are now centered in technology and social media — modes that are far beyond what I can embrace and grow into. As a result, communication to and from me has become less reliable. Today's world of birth has moved beyond my abilities and my comfort zone.

After 40 years glorying in the wonder of this raw and elemental power, it is time to let it pass to the new generation of midwives. May they warm themselves in the glow of new life.

Note: Karen Ehrlich began her journey with birth in 1972 and retired from clinical care in 2015. She hopes that this memoir will ecourage other long-time midwives to write their stories, so the many-layered tapestry of the re-emergence of midwifery will be available for generations to come. She is married and is a stepmother, grandmother, and great-grandmother, aunt and great-aunt. Her Master's thesis, completed in 2003, is entitled *"Life Is a Sexually Transmitted Condition: The Sexuality of Labor and Birth."* It can be read online at midwifekaren.org

Chapter 11: My Hip Santa Cruz History
by Dan Phillips

Our family lived in Berkeley from 1968 to 1971 during the tumultuous Vietnam protest years. I taught English at Merritt College, home of the Black Panthers, in the Oakland ghetto flatlands. In 1971, I joined my students on strike to protest the closing of our college in favor of a new one in the predominantly white Oakland hills. Consequently, I narrowly escaped being beaten and arrested in the ensuing police-incited riot at the old Merritt and subsequently, quit my job. After that incident and everything happening in Berkeley at that time, my wife and I began planning our escape from a country under Nixon we believed was becoming a fascist enclave.

So, we rented out the house and were on and off the road for six months, all the way up to British Columbia. There our "back to the land, "new community" dream came to an abortive end in the middle of the winter of '72 when a record twelve feet of snow trapped us in our one-room cabin and made us realize this rugged lifestyle was too far out for us. Returning home to Berkeley, but still longing to leave, in 1973 we found an old Russian River resort with eleven cabins and a house slowly mouldering under an acre of redwoods in Monte Rio, a small town, rural compromise only 75 miles away from San Francisco. It could provide us with a home and livelihood, so we sold our Berkeley home and moved again.

After holding onto the resort through fire and flood for five years, we greatly missed the cultural advantages of the Bay Area that included good schools for our two daughters. Less dense and tumultuous than Berkeley with a rich counterculture of its own, Santa Cruz, where my wife's younger sister lived with her family, seemed like the perfect place to live.

1978 was a renaissance time in Santa Cruz with everyone acting out their dreams and experimenting in new directions. I took improv performance at Cabrillo and began my acting career with local auteur and Hollywood film maker, Dan Bessie, starring in his production of "The World of Sholom Aleichem". Then I performed as a sax-playing, rapper for the Master USA Contest sponsored by the Screaming Memes for the local Woman's Caucus in a hilarious parody of the Miss America pageant.

After taking acting and improv classes at Cabrillo from Judy Slattum and Wilma Marcus, I began doing stand-up comedy on Wednesday amateur nights at the Art Center in downtown Santa Cruz, preparing weekly bits as a Jewish Rastafarian with a skullcap and corn-row braids, and a Polish sewer worker, complete with hip boots and three-pronged fork, running for president who promised to "fork" President Reagan out of Washington. Forming a comedy group with other amateurs, I booked a successful performance at U.C. Davis. My short lived comedy career ended, however, with my performance at the also short-lived Copabanana comedy club in Capitola where I made the mistake of performing the "Three Hugs a Day" bit I learned in Judy Slattum's class and incurred the wrath of the owner who, unbeknownst to me, as the originator of Hug Therapy, thought I was satirizing him. Ralph Peduto, well known local impresario, local actor and Hollywood extra who had booked the gig, vehemently declared I would never "work in this town again!" although I did act in his play "Where's the Kitchen". Undaunted, I went on to act in local theater groups like Mountain Community Theater in their first production, "Happy Birthday Wanda June" and Cabrillo College in Wilma Marcus' production of "A View from the Bridge". With Irv Washkov I formed the Trumbinikehs, at Temple Beth El and produced and performed in numerous Jewish-themed plays.

Everyone seemed to be into some form of self-improvement therapy, and I was no exception. I'll never forget a hypnotherapy group that was an off-shoot of the Men's Sex and Power therapy where I role-played an angry father belittling his son who had to be restrained by four men from throttling me. Some years later when I chanced to meet the "son", he warmly thanked me for the long-term effects of reducing his incapacitating rage. Now, mainly for fun and companionship, I've been in a monthly men's drumming circle for the past twenty-five some years.

In 1980, I went back to my old love of teaching poetry as an independent contractor, partially subsidizing elementary, middle and high schools to bring me into the classroom through California Arts Council grants, first as a poet in the statewide California Poets-in-the-Schools program and then hired with Patrice Vecchione as the first two poets under the Santa Cruz County Arts Council's SPECTRA program. For roughly three years from, 1980 to 1983, I conducted over thirty student workshops in over twenty different elementary, junior high and high schools in Santa Cruz county plus a few in Monterey county.

My Santa Cruz "mind-blowing" experiences were coming as a result of seeing kids turn on to poetry and write their first poems. As early as first grade, I'd ask the kids with their limited written vocabulary to write name poems with lines beginning with a letter of their first name that contained a thing or a person they liked. Each workshop day, I gave the students an exercise that would elicit a poem and with every workshop, a book of their poems would be published followed by a reading event to celebrate their creative spirits. I also gave regular classroom teachers training to provide continuity for their students after my workshops ended.

I have always felt it was my loving duty to give students an immediate creative outlet to express their feelings and desires free of the restrictive emphasis on correct grammar and syntax, as a supplement and not a replacement for the correct writing skills they must learn in the public school. Most importantly, I wanted to make writing enjoyable and give them that all-important feeling of accomplishment and personal validation for their creative efforts.

However, even though my wife was working, I soon found that teaching poetry didn't bring in enough to support our family. So, until I found a regular junior college English teaching job, my original vocation in the '60's and '70's, I began selling vegetables to restaurants from a wholesaler in Santa Cruz. Then, I went to work for a Swiss company with a gourmet line of chocolate and bakery products, serving hotels, bakeries and restaurants from Burlingame to Carmel including Santa Cruz.

Also, in the food line, I taught a chocolate tasting class at Cabrillo where I converted Hershey eaters to the gourmet European chocolate cause, threw parties where I shaved thin slices off kilo blocks of dark and white to melt on the tongues of numerous friends and relatives, and handed out my own specially designed boxes of English chocolate mints at Christmas. Gaining unlooked for notoriety, I became known as "Dan Dan the chocolate man".

Meanwhile, enjoying "shmoosing" with the chefs for my Swiss products, I soon hit on the idea of procuring for them whatever gourmet items their regular suppliers didn't carry—baby vegetables, local goat cheese, caviar, smoked fish, duck and specialty game. I seduced Carmel chefs and restaurant owners into buying my chocolate after bringing them fresh herbs from an organic farm near Stanford. But soon, I found burning too much rubber in a job that wasn't paying enough was also rapidly burning me out!

Finally, in 1990, I secured a regular position at San José City, where I taught English composition, literature and creative writing for ten years till I retired at 62. Then I volunteered as a poetry teacher in my grandsons' classrooms at Gault and Pacific Elementary and, most recently, assisted in the county's Young Writers Program at Branciforte Junior High.

As a writer and teacher, I have not only benefitted hundreds of students but also promoted poetry in Santa Cruz county. Together with Phil Wagner, a dedicated, celebrated local poet, we launched the Bookshop Santa Cruz on-going poetry series under the aegis of the National Writers' Union for five years before Poetry Santa Cruz took over. I have also been honored to have many of my own poems published locally in magazines and literary reviews such as Porter Gulch Review, phren-z, Catamaran, Monterey Bay Poetry Review and Homestead Review and given readings at Bookshop Santa Cruz, Capitola Book Café, East Village Café, Porter Library, Santa Cruz Library, UCSC Chadwick Garden and Cabrillo College. Additionally, I have self-published a poetry and prose memoir of Bali, The Bali in Me, in homage to that place where I became a dedicated artist, and a chapbook of poetry also inspired by my travels called Places of the Spirit. Recently, I have completed a full-length book of my collected poetry. Also, over the years since coming to Santa Cruz, I have completed two, as yet, unpublished novels.

For twenty years, we owned a second home in Bali to which I have had the pleasure of introducing scores of Santa Cruzans along with others from Hawaii, Europe, Asia, Canada and Australia to that natural and cultural paradise. Renting and exchanging our Bali and Santa Cruz homes with people in Hawaii, Baja California, Arizona, New Mexico, Miami Beach,

New York, London, Paris and Normandy has enabled my wife and I to see the world.

As long as I've been in Santa Cruz, I've had a semi-professional musical career. I have played jazz and Jewish Klezmer with my saxophone and clarinet for numerous events as well as contracted my musical aggregations to play in clubs, cafés, restaurants and for private celebrations at various locations throughout the county. In 1990, I joined the new Balinese gamelan at UCSC taught by Linda Burman-Hall and played for the succeeding ten years in regular concerts and special events around Santa Cruz and the San Francisco Bay Area. With Linda and other "Baliophiles", we formed a Bali friendship group to promote Balinese culture with musical performances and classes in Balinese arts and crafts. In the 2000's I went back to school to study theory, composition and improvisational performance with the master teacher, Ray Brown, and played for a brief time with the Cabrillo Jazz band conducted by Jon Norgren.

What truly makes Santa Cruz "hip" for me is the value it places on the arts and the warm, receptive and supportive home it makes for its artists.

I consider myself fortunate to have come at a time when the arts in Santa Cruz were flourishing. You couldn't help dancing up the Pacific Garden Mall to the sounds of Don McCaslin and his group outside the old Cooper House on your way to Bookshop Santa Cruz. Then you could take the book of your choice to Caffe Pergolesi run by our old friends from the '60's in San Francisco's North Beach, Judy and Frank Foreman, for a cappucino, and see most everyone you knew or cared to meet, and maybe even be stimulated enough by the potent combination of good caffeine, literature and conversation to write a poem. Since that renaissance time in '78, I have done most creative work here for 42 years. Hopefully, I will keep on for many more!

Chapter 12: The Hip Pocket Bookstore Obscenity Case
by Stanley D. Stevens

Content:
1. Chronology and Description of the Incident
2. Transcriptions of *Santa Cruz Sentinel* newspaper articles
3. Decision of Judge Harry F. Brauer
4. Interview of Judge Brauer by Wally Trabing, *Santa Cruz Sentinel* Columnist
5. Disclaimer of author

---

1. Chronology and Description of the Incident

• On August 5, 1965, Peter Arnon Demma, Manager of the Hip Pocket Book Store, expressed his views on obscenity, in a letter to the Editor of the Santa Cruz Sentinel.

• On October 29, 1965, Ron Reeves, Sentinel Staff Writer, reported that Peter Demma and Ronald Bevirt had been arrested for displaying photographs taken by Walter Chappell. The exhibit included a group of pictures, a variety of subjects ranging from intricate leaf studies to photos of male genitalia and anal regions.

• On November 1, 1965, the Board of Directors of the Santa Cruz County Chapter of the A.C.L.U. met in its regular meeting at the home of Dr. Duncan Holbert. Elizabeth Moore, Secretary, recorded the proceedings (in part) as follows:

"The meeting was called to order by chairman Dan Miller.

"Stan Stevens introduced Peter Demma and Ron Bevrit [sic], owners of the Hip Pocket Book Store, who described the harassment to which they have been subjected by certain elements in the community. Stan Stevens conjectured as to what kind of action we could initiate to oppose this harassment and the groups behind it. After some discussion Dr. Holbert moved, with John Lingemann seconding, that we form a committee to determine what legal procedure can be taken to deal quickly and responsibly in this matter to represent our interests and that the committee be given the authority to act according to its conclusions. The motion carried. The committee was appointed and consists of the following: Dan Miller, Stan Stevens, Ian McPhail and Myra McLoughlin.

"A discussion of questionable police actions followed with John Garvison suggesting that complaints relating to these be written up that include all of the facts. A committee was formed to develop a program of education and liason [sic] in dealing with law enforcement authorities. The committee is composed of the following: Ann Read, John Lingemann, Peter Beagle and Margaret Lezin. Peter Demma volunteered, as a non-board member, to serve on this committee. Margaret Lezin was appointed chairman."

• On December 6, 1965, the Board of Directors of the Santa Cruz County Chapter of the A.C.L.U. met in its regular meeting at the home of Dr. Duncan Holbert. Elizabeth Moore, Secretary, recorded the proceedings (in part) as follows:

"The meeting was called to order by chairman Dan Miller.

"Stan Stevens reported that the committee that was appointed to take action on the Hip Pocket case did not function since the Northern Calif. Board assumed responsibility for the initiation of action, securing the services of Bob Bennett for the defense of Peter Demma and Ron Bevirt.

"Stan Stevens submitted letters of appreciation that he had written to Bob Bennett and Bruce Richardson on behalf of our board. A discussion followed regarding the wording and proper recipients of the letters and it was decided to have the secretary rewrite them to the firm of Wyckoff, Parker, Boyle & Pope of Watsonville, expressing our appreciation for their cooperation in the form of the donation of Mr. Bennett's and Mr. Richardson's services toward the successful defense of the Hip Pocket case.

"Stan Stevens commented that Judge Brauer's explanation of his decision on the case was to be highly commended for its excellence and conjectured whether we could get it printed and distributed. After discussing this possibility, the board vetoed the idea."

---

2. Transcriptions of Santa Cruz Sentinel newspaper articles

1965 Aug 5 p. 19
STORE MANAGER TELLS VIEWS ON OBSCENITY
[To the] Editor: Many in the community are anxious to learn what we at the Hip Pocket Bookstore consider to be obscenity.

In answer to this may we state that we feel that when a minister devotes time to reading erotic literary passages to women members of his flock in the interests of "combatting Satan," that this is obscenity.

And when persons buy for other than literary purposes many nudist magazines and erotic works to fill a sack to be delivered to Lord knows where when their money might better have been spent buying salve for Vietnamese children's napalm burns, that this is obscenity.

If those who feel civicly responsible enough to lash out at something endangering our youth then why is not boredom, the real corruptor, attacked?

Many of our detractors who feel they are warring against human degradation cannot realize that we are on their side of this war. We believe, however, that the war against human degradation cannot be won by cultivating neurosis, and by neurosis we mean dreadful pre-occupation.

We have a good book on our shelves called "Passion and Social Constrait"[sic; i.e., Passion and Social Constraint. By Ernest Van Den Haag, in association with Ralph Ross (New York: Stein and Day, 1963)] which does a good job of bringing the reader out of "Tannhauser" into the light of the current situation.

We suggest that those who believe us to be "minions of the Devil" sit right down and read this book.

Peter Arnon Demma
Manager, Hip Pocket Bookstore
1520 Pacific avenue

1965 Oct 29 p. 1
SC Pair To Face Obscenity Rap
by Ron Reeves, Sentinel Staff Writer

The uproar over whether or not certain pictures included in a photographic display at the Hip Pocket book store are obscene or art has led to the arrest of the shop's two owners.

Peter A. Demma, 28, of 227 Union street, and his partner, Ronald K. Bevirt, 26, who said he lives at the store at 1520 Pacific avenue, were released on their own recognizance yesterday.

They were arraigned on three charges each this morning and the matters were continued to November 18 at 10 a.m. for entry of pleas.

The pictures, which were taken by a nationally known photographer, Walter Chappell of Taos, New Mexico, have been under scrutiny by authorities since they went up at the book store some three weeks ago. Chappell, who is now living at Big Sur, exhibited a group of pictures, which included a variety of subjects, ranging from intricate leaf studies to photos of male genitalia and anal regions.

The pictures raised the ire of the city police department and many citizens. Outraged viewers staged a telephone barrage of complaints directed at the police, district attorney and the book store itself.

District Attorney Richard Pease had the matter under study and was researching laws which might apply when city police went directly to municipal court yesterday afternoon, obtained a warrant, arrested the two owners and confiscated five of the pictures.

The men are facing three misdemeanor charges of knowingly exhibiting obscene matter, knowingly possessing obscene matter which could be seen by minors and outraging public decency.

Police Chief Geno Pini said: "In our opinion, this material was totally and completely obscene in the manner in which it was displayed. It was totally and utterly without redeeming social importance and those are the words that the state law uses to define a violation of this law. Many, many people agree with our opinion in this matter."

District Attorney Pease this morning said the question of whether the pictures are art or obscenities "will be the issue, really."

"There will be a substantial number of people who will testify that they were outraged," Pease stated.

Pease said he was aware of the pictures and had requested the shop operators to remove them. They went down for a while, by coincidence while the gallery portion of the shop was being painted and then went back up.

"I had discussed it with the police department and the principle [sic] problem is finding a statute to cover the kind of activity which took place here," Pease said.

Now that the pair have been arrested, Pease and his staff will handle prosecution in the matter.

Demma said he definitely does not consider the pictures to be obscene.

"The quality of the photography could hardly be considered obscene regardless of what is depicted," Demma stated.

Chief Pini, on the other hand said: "The focal point of the photographs are male genitalia, anal areas and so forth. The photographs certainly do not encompass the entire human form."

A check of the bookshop this morning showed the police did not confiscate other photos showing female breasts and pubic zones.

Demma said Pease "advised us to take some move to quell the public anger." Demma said he did not consider the exhibit to be out of line and left if up despite "thousands" of telephone calls.

"A very few people objected repeatedly," said his partner, Bevirt.

Bevirt indicated that he has contacted an attorney, Marshall Krause, who has worked with the American Civil Liberties union.

Bevirt explained at length his reasons for believing the pictures in question are not obscene.

"I do not believe the naked human body and its parts are obscene. I believe that the whole concept of obscenity is a symptom of the societal illness which we have passed on for a long time by means of sexual guilt," he said.

1965 Nov 5 p. 12
Obscenity Case Transferred To Watsonville

Peter A. Demma, 28, and Ronald K. Bevirt, 26, co-owners of the Hip Pocket book store, appeared in Municipal court this morning to answer three misdemeanor charges involving the display of photos which police have branded as "obscene."

Attorney Robert Bennett, who represented the pair, told the court he will make some motions in the case which may require considerable legal argument.

Judge James J. Scoppettone, because of his heavy court schedule, referred the matter to Watsonville Municipal court. A tentative appearance date of November 12 was set.

Demma and Bevirt were arrested October 28 by city police after they obtained a Municipal court warrant. They are facing charges of knowingly exhibiting obscene matter, knowingly possessing obscene matter which could be seen by minors and outraging public decency.

Police confiscated five pictures from the bookstore. They were by Walter Chappell of Taos, New Mexico, a nationally known photographer who currently lives in Big Sur.

The arrests came after numerous people complained to authorities about the pictures.

District Attorney Richard Pease, in charge of prosecuting the matter, said the question will be whether the pictures are legally considered to be obscenities or art.

1965 Nov 10 p. 5
Book Store Owners To Seek Dismissal Of Obscenity Case

Motions will be made to Watsonville Municipal court judge Harry Brauer on Friday, November 26, in the obscenity case involving the co-owners of the Hip Pocket book store here.

Peter A. Demma, 28, and Ronald K. Bevirt, 26, appeared Monday before Judge Brauer with Atty. Robert Bennett. They requested time on November 26 to present motins to have the cases dismissed.

The three charges involve photographs by Walter Chappel of Taos, New Mexico, which were displayed in an exhibit at the book store. City police obtained a warrant and had the men arrested October 28.

They are specifically charged with knowingly exhibiting obscene matter, knowingly possessing obscene matter which could be seen by minors and outraging public decency.

The motions will present evidence for a decision of law in attempts to have the pictures ruled not to be obscene and therefore to dismiss the charges. As yet the men have not entered pleas, but have publicly declared they do not feel the pictures are obscene.

1965 Nov 23 p. 3
Obscenity Hearing Reset For 10 A.M. On Friday

Watsonville Municipal Court Judge Harry Brauer has allowed more time to hear motions in the obscenity proceedings brought against the owners of the Hip Pocket bookstore of Santa Cruz.

Peter A. Demma, 28, and Ronald K. Bevirt, 26, were charged by city police concerning five photographs included in an exhibit at the store. The police also confiscated the five pictures in question.

The motions originally were set to be heard Friday at 2 p.m. Judge Braurer, after a conference with District Attorney Richard Pease and Robert Bennett, an attorney representing the pair, reset the matter for Friday at 10 a.m.

The judge has before him motions requesting that the charges be dismissed because the pictures are not obscene under law. There also is a motion declaring that the pictures were illegally confiscated and asking for their return.

The photos, taken by Walter Chappell of Taos, New Mexico, have been declared obscene by police. The shop owners declare they are not. Witnesses, said to include art teachers, are to testify Friday concerning their opinions. The photos dwell mainly with male genitalia and anal regions.

The charges against the shop owners are knowingly exhibiting obscene matter, knowingly possessing obscene matter which could be seen by minors and outraging public decency.

1965 Nov 28 p. 3:1-8
Judge Dismisses Santa Cruz Obscene Photo Charge
by Ron Reeves, Sentinel Staff Writer

Photographs which police seized from the Hip Pocket book store may or may not be art, but they are not legally obscene.

So ruled Watsonville Municipal Court Judge Harry Brauer Friday afternoon when he dismissed two charges facing the shop's owners, Peter Demma and Ronald Bevirt. The unusual pre-trial hearing is provided by law in obscenity cases which compel a judge to rule whether or not the material is obscene. The hearing came before either of the defendants was required to enter a plea.

Although the photos, taken by nationally known photographer Walter Chappell of Taos, New Mexico, are not legally acceptable, they will not be returned to the shop's gallery. Bevirt said the

Chappell show has completed its time limit and another exhibit is ready to go up.

Several witnesses testified in defense of the photos, which included shots of nude male and female forms — with emphasis on the male sexual organs. The general trend of the testimony was that art can be art through the handling of the media used, regardless of the subject depicted. The testimony also pointed out that the confiscated photos were only a part of an entire show, and should not be considered out of context.

The only private citizen testifying against the photos was Robert Husband, president of the Santa Cruz Art league. Husband declared that the pictures are "ordinary," "quite ordinary," and "very ordinary" and not much as far as art is concerned.

"I wouldn't consider it great art; I wouldn't pay any money for it," said Husband. He testified that he is a collector of the old masters and has little leaning toward modern or abstract art. He also testified that he doesn't know of any artists who "value" abstract works.

Attorneys for the defendants, Robert Bennett and Bruce Richardson, stressed that a higher level of art is depicted by the photographs, that of shape, form, texture and composition.

Dr. Arthur Giese, a Santa Cruz psychiatrist, said: "This particular material would not arouse the prurient interest of the average person," when asked for his opinion. He admitted, however, that he considered the pictures to be "unusual" and hadn't seen any similar photos displayed in Santa Cruz or elsewhere.

Leon Taborly [*i.e.*, Tabory], a Santa Cruz clinical psychologist, said he considered the Chappell photos to have a "very reverent attitude towards natural forces and forms." He indicated he could see nothing pornographic in them, knew Chappell personally, and considered his purpose in making the photos on a much higher plane.

Rev. John David Arnold of Ben Lomond, an Episcopal worker priest, said: "I quite frankly had a poetic reaction when I saw them."

Demma took the stand to introduce the remainder of the photo exhibit to the court and to explain that it had been shown at San

Francisco State college and at Big Sur.

Judge Brauer gave an extensive presentation when making his ruling that legally the pictures could not be considered to be obscene.

He based his decision on the First Amendment to the Constitution, which provides for freedom of speech, and said it is considered to be the "cornerstone of our law."

"It is true, of course, that obscenity, as such, is not protected by the court," the judge told some 75 persons who sat through the hearing.

He said, however, that the law makes it clear that only "hard core pornography" can be confiscated or suppressed.

He said the legal definition of hard core pornography includes three points. They are that "to the average person, applying contemporary standards, the predominant appeal of the matter, taken as a whole, is to prurient interest, i.e., a shameful or morbid interest in nudity, sex or excretion."

The second point is that the material "goes substantially beyond customary limits of candor in description or representation of such matters." The third point is that the matter is "utterly without redeeming social importance.

The judge explained that, to be declared obscene, the material in question must fall under all three categories. He felt the pictures did not, and therefore dismissed the charges against the two men. They had been accused of displaying obscene matter and displaying obscene matter where it could be viewed by minors.

The judge also held that other material introduced by the defendants, including nudist magazines and pulp books purchased in the county, were of a lower quality than the photos.

"The defendants have introduced magazines available at any drug store which are unquestionably more arousing than any of the five pictures," the judge said.

"The exhibits are not hard core pornography and they are therefore not obscene," he declared.

The matter came to the court after numerous complaints about the exhibit reached the city police and district attorney's office.

Captain Richard Overton testified that he, Police Chief Geno Pini and Assistant Chief Ernest Marenghi decided to bypass District Attorney Richard Pease, who wanted additional legal study before moving in the case.

"He (Pease) asked for further time to review Supreme Court decisions in the matter and look into it further . . . We wanted to bring it to a head, and we did," Captain Overton testified.

The matter was taken to City Attorney Rod Atchison, who drew up the complaint at the request of the police department. The complaint was used to arrest the men and confiscate the pictures. The matter then went to Pease for prosecution.

1970 Jun 7 p. 12 cont. on p. 13:1
Honors For Robert Husband

Wednesday marks the opening of an unusual one-man show of charcoal and pencil drawings at the Santa Cruz Art League, 526 Broadway. This special exhibit, direct from deSaisset Museum of Art at Santa Clara University, will be on display in the Ella Gray Gallery until the end of June.

The artist, Robert M. Husband of Santa Cruz, a past president of the Santa Cruz Art League, is a permanent exhibitor at deSaisset Museum in Santa Clara, where the Robert M. Husband Gallery was dedicated last night. His most recent achievement, exhibited for the first time at the dedication, is a series of musical instruments and the hands that play them done in charcoal, entitled "The Hands of the Symphony Orchestra." The artist used members of the Santa Cruz Symphony Orchestra as models.

When, in his teens, Robert Husband was faced with the choice of a career, an emotional tug-of-war between art and engineering ensued. Engineering won, and he was graduated from the University of Illinois with a degree in mechanical engineering four years later. His career has included such positions as dollar-a-year man on the War Production Board in World War II, civilian aide to the Chief of Army Ordnance, for which he received a citation, an expert consultant to Reconstruction Finance Corporation in

Washington, and a top executive of Consolidated Machine Tool Corporation of Rochester, New York, builders of the world's largest metal-working machinery.

In 1960 he retired, came to Santa Cruz, and resumed his old love of drawing with pencil and charcoal. He has exhibited extensively in California and while he is at liberty to exhibit when and where he chooses, the Robert M. Husband Gallery in Santa Clara is now the permanent home of this unique collection of fine art.

The public is invited to visit the one-man show in the Ella Gray Gallery, as well as the new June exhibit of member artist paintings in the Margaret Rogers Gallery. Hours are 1 to 5 p.m. daily. Hours for the Last Supper Gallery in the same building continue as in the past at 10 a.m. to 5 p.m. There is no admission charge for any of these exhibits.

Next Sunday, June 14, the Santa Cruz Art League will honor Robert Husband with a tea from 2 to 4 p.m. with the public invited to attend.

---

3. *Decision of Judge Harry F. Brauer*

[Transcribed and Annotated from a photocopy in the files of the author.]

```
    Harry F. Brauer, Judge Municipal Court of the
Santa Cruz Judicial District, County of Santa
Cruz, State of California, Department No. 2
    Case No. CR 13868 The People of the State of
California, Plaintiffs, vs. Peter A. Demma and
Ronald K. Bevirt, Defendants.
    Santa Cruz, Santa Cruz, California) · 7 Jun
1970, Sun Page 12 Downloaded on Mar 5, 2019
Robert Reporter's Transcript, by Roy E. June,
a Certified Shorthand Reporter, [under the
supervision of] Robert V. Hughes, C.S.R., Official
Court Reporter, Santa Cruz, California.
    Watsonville, California, November 26, 1965,
Honorable Harry F. Brauer, Presiding.
    Appearances: Richard J. Pease, Esq., District
```

Attorney of the Santa Cruz County, for the People.

Robert L. Bennett, Esq., and Bruce A. Richardson, Esq., for the Defendants, of the firm, Wyckoff, Parker, Boyle & Pope, Esqs.

THE COURT: Because this case is a rather important one and has obviously aroused the emotions of a substantial segment of the community, pro or con, I propose to detail at some length the applicable law, the reasons for the Court's ruling, because I think it is generally of benefit if the reasons for judicial decisions are articulated so people can understand them.

In a case of this sort we start with the Constitution of the United States. In fact, we start not only with the Constitution, which for many, many years has been regarded as the cornerstone of our law. It is by express and multiple decisions of our highest court the most important section of the Constitution. So much so that if there are any rights protected by any other provisions of the constitution that conflict with a right protected by the First Amendment, the First Amendment right prevails. And, of course, I am referring specifically to that provision which states: "Congress shall make no law abridging the freedom of speech." And this provision has for many, many years been held applicable to the states as well.

Because freedom of speech is the cornerstone of our law the book seller, the book store, is a unique enterprise in that it enjoys greater protection than any other enterprise, with the possible exception of a newspaper or magazine.

Our Supreme Court in a recent decision which was mentioned earlier this morning, the Marcus case [Marcus v. Search Warrant, 367 U.S. 717 (1961)], has gone into a detailed historical analysis of the First Amendment, the freedom of speech provision, and really it would be of benefit to all citizens if they could read it [https://en.wikipedia.org/wiki/Marcus_v._Search_Warrant].

The Court started with an analysis of conditions obtaining in 16th Century England when the obscenity laws, coupled with the law against libel and sedition were lumped together and employed as a device to suppress all dissenters. This was very simple, that on the mere decision of some official a book seller's stock could be seized, impounded, and, of course, the man was out of business. Gradually amelioration of this system went into effect and slowly, case by case, these laws were bridged and the general warrant, the notorious general warrants then invoked were abrogated.

The point is that our founders were poignantly aware of the history of these sedition and obscenity laws when they drafted that incredibly marvelous document, our Constitution. Just this noon I came across a little quotation which I would like to share with you: "I am mortified to be told that in the United States of America a question about the sale of a book can be carried before the magistrate. Are we to have a censor whose imprimatur shall say what book may be sold and what we may buy? Shall a layman, simple as ourselves, set up his reason as the rule for what we are to read? It is an insult to our citizens to question whether they are rational actions or not." This was not written by some contemporary radical, but by Thomas Jefferson.

Because freedom of speech enjoys such a preferred position in our legal hierarchy the conditions under which utterances, whether in the form of books or pictures, may be suppressed are stringently limited in the law. It is true, of course, that obscenity as such is not protected by the Constitution. Nor for that matter is deformation, nor is advocacy of the violent overthrow of our form of government. But the law makes clear that only hard-core pornography qualifies for suppression. And anything short of hard-core pornography enjoys Constitutional protection.

Consistent with that Constitutional rule the California Legislature has enacted Section 311 of the Penal Code. And Section 311 sets forth three standards which apply before a particular work of literature or art may be suppressed and the exhibitor or owner criminally prosecuted. And all three factors must exist in a particular case before the matter may be suppressed or may be determined to be obscene. And, incidentally, it is also because the First Amendment is in such a preferred position that we even have this hearing for which there is no statutory sanction. This comes straight from the Constitution as interpreted by the high court. Namely, before the question of obscenity may ever be submitted to a jury in a trial the Court must make a preliminary determination as to whether the matter is obscene or not. And if the Court rules that it is not obscene the case must be dismissed. If the Court rules that it is obscene, then the Court's judgment may still be overruled by a jury. And a jury, of course, must in addition find the person charged knew that the matter was obscene.

Now, the three elements of the California Obscenity Statute are these: "One, that to the average person, applying contemporary standards, the predominant appeal of the matter, taken as a whole is to prurient interest, that is, a shameful or morbid interest in nudity, sex, or excretion." The second criterion is: "That it must go substantially beyond customary limits of candor in description or representation." And the third is: "That the matter must be utterly" — and that has been defined to mean completely

— "without redeeming social importance." Unless an utterance fits into all three of these pigeon holes it may not be deemed to be obscene.

Now, in the light of that statutory criterion let us view the exhibits here, specifically the five items which were seized by the police. I am certainly not an artist. If this were a book I would consider myself far more qualified to make an independent determination. One of the five I can't even tell what it is. But we have had witnesses here, and I noticed that several of the witnesses, Mr. Husband for instance [Robert M. Husband,(1892-1974) President of the Santa Cruz Art League] and some of the witnesses for the defense, turned it upside down when looking at it, or sideways. I can hardly believe that that particular picture arouses prurient interests in anybody. I didn't even know what it was. The others contain — well, they all contain representations of nudity, in some instances of sex organs. Mr. Pease [District Attorney Richard J. Pease], who has, however, tried a case before me once involving hard-core obscenity and pictures that were hardcore obscenity doubtless sees the difference between these pictures and hard-core obscenity. I don't know whether the appeal of these pictures is to prurient interests. The art experts have indicated that the predominant appeal is not. In any event, defendants have introduced magazines which are obtainable here in any drugstore and which unquestionable are far, far more arousing than these particular five pictures, sexually arousing, if you will. This is, of course, relevant in that the second criterion is that the matter must go substantially beyond customary limits of candor, and I don't rest my decision particularly on that ground, because I would be very unhappy to think that what you can find in a liquor store represents the community standard.

The third ground, however, here is the crucial one, as I see it. The law states that in order for a representation to be obscene it must be utterly without redeeming social importance, and that means it must be completely without artistic value. The criterion is not, as the Zeitlin case [Zeitlin v. Arnebergh: L.A. No. 26905. In Bank, California Supreme Court, July 2, 1963.] made clear, that if the prurient interest in the matter exceeds its artistic merit it is obscene. The criterion is that the matter must be entirely without artistic interest. In other words, it must be hard-core pornography in order to be labeled obscene.

Now, we have heard from artists, from art teachers, from a psychiatrist [Dr. Arthur Giese of Santa Cruz], from a minister [Rev. John David Arnold of Ben Lomond, an Episcopal worker priest], from a clinical psychologist [Leon Tabory], all of whom see artistic merit in these pictures, especially if viewed as a whole, and under the statute they must be viewed as a whole, that is, in context with the other pictures in the exhibit. The photographer [Walter Chappell of Taos, NM] is one who has received national recognition. I note that the People's witness, Mr. Husband, who is a very frank witness, has really not contradicted to any significant extent the testimony of the other witnesses, other than to say that in his subjective judgment it isn't art. Well, in my judgment it may not be, either. But that is not the statutory criterion. My views on the matter, for that matter, do not count, either. It is the function of a trial judge to apply the law as it exists and the Constitutional law of the United States as interpreted by its highest court. That is, of course, binding upon me.

As judged by these criteria the exhibits are not hard-core pornography. They are not, therefore, obscene as defined in Section 311. They must be returned to the owner and this action will be dismissed.

[Note: Blanks below are not filled-in my photocopy of the Decision.]

STATE OF CALIFORNIA)
) ss.
COUNTY OF SANTA CRUZ)

I, ROY E. JUNE, a Certified Shorthand Reporter in and for the State of California, do hereby certify that on the _____ day of _____, 1965, I fully, truly, and correctly took down in stenotype all of the proceedings had and all the testimony given in the above-entitled court in the case of THE PEOPLE OF THE STATE OF CALIFORNIA, Plaintiff, versus PETER A. DEMMA and RONALD K. BEVIRT, Defendants, and numbered pages 1 to 8, inclusive, in the files of Civil Actions in said court;

That I reported and said proceedings fully and correctly; and that the foregoing pages are a full, true, complete and correct transcription of my stenotype notes taken at said time and place, prepared under my direction and supervision.

4. Interview of Judge Brauer

by Wally Trabing, *Santa Cruz Sentinel* Columnist
Source: *Santa Cruz Sentinel* December 14, 1965, p. 2:3-4.

Mostly about People by Wally Trabing
The First Amendment ... And Pornography

Judge Harry F. Brauer's not-guilty decision in the recent Hip Pocket Book store obscenity case involving several "art" photographs — was not a popular one.

He would not discuss it until he was satisfied his decision would not be appealed. He was satisfied last week and I sat down with him to get home some important points.

Emotionally I was one who wanted to see a guilty verdict, but intellectually I think Judge Brauer was wise, and that his decision was right.

The judge told me he had spent a great many hours briefing himself on obscenity laws and cases. Even though "four out of the five photographs (using parts of the body in abstract 'still life' photography) were disgusting to me," he could see no other decision to make.

"In the middle 16th century, a law was enacted in England giving the king or whoever was in authority, the power to search any house and to seize any material which, in the opinion of the messenger or policeman, was seditious, obscene, heretical, or libelous — and burn it.

"Any dissent from the accepted doctrine, religiously or politically, was suppressed. This law was carried to America in the colonial days.

"Our founders were so poignantly aware of this danger to individual rights, that they enacted the First Amendment," he said.

The amendments are generally called the Bill of Rights, and they were submitted (the first 10) to the first Congress in 1789 to clarify certain individual and state rights not named in the Constitution.

The First Amendment reads as follows: "Congress shall make no law respecting an establishment of religion, or prohibiting the free exercise thereof; or abridging the freedom of speech or of the press; or the right of people peaceably to assemble and to petition the government for a redress of grievances."

Judge Brauer said that through the years book stores, newspapers, all forms of expression, have enjoyed more protection than anything else.

"So much so that only three exceptions are recognized by the courts: 1. That which is designed incite to [sic] the violent overthrow of the government. 2. Libel or slander. 3. Hard core pornography."

The definition of pornography was set by the Supreme Court in 1957 (Roth case) and adopted by the California legislature in 1961.

It says that to be pornographic or obscene, material must flunk three "tests":

1. To the average person, applying contemporary standards, the predominant appeal of the material, taken as a whole, is to those with a shameful or morbid interest in nudity, sex, or excretion.

2. Material which goes substantially beyond customary limits of candor in description or representation of such matters.

3. Material which is utterly without redeeming social importance.

"This is tough when carried out to the letter of the law. A piece of material or photo may flunk two "tests" but this isn't enough," he said.

What can be done to get rid of the trash, then?

"As far as I can see, nothing can be done to broaden the area of suppression under the Constitution as interpreted by the highest court," said Brauer.

"A wise federal judge, whose name is William Mathes, once said: "The rights of good men are secure only so long as the rights of bad people are also protected."

"Please note," he said, "that Demma and Bevirt of the Hip Pocket are not bad people. I brought this quote up as an example of the theory behind the First Amendment."

"I realize all this is frustrating. You can point out the same frustration with crime in general.

'Sure we must combat crime, but if we use the thumbscrew and rack we could combat it better, but this would be spitting on the American flag," said Judge Brauer.

"One thing that could be done would be to pass legislation barring access of certain material to minors," he said.

So this is the crux of the question.

There is "hard core" pornography and people are being jailed for it or possessing it.

There is plenty of disgusting and filthy material around that must be protected by our Constitution to protect the over-all freedom; the publishing world is crawling with the ilk who earn their keep by it.

There's no law which says you cannot express yourself loud and clear against what you think is disgusting.

There's no law that says you have to buy it or look at it.

---

5. *Disclaimer of Author*

Nothing in this article is intended by the author/transcriber as being a statement of Current Law on any of the subjects discussed. We must remember that this case was decided in 1965. There may have been changes in the California law on pornography, although it is not the intent of this article to explore that possiblity. Nothing in this article is intended to give legal advice, since the author is not an attorney. Anyone who faces a similar circumstance as what Peter Demma and Ronald Bevirt faced in 1965, should contact a representative of the American Civil Liberties Union, Santa Cruz Chapter, or the attorneys at the Northern California ACLU in San Francisco.

Chapter 13: Melyssa Demma: The First 8 years
Interviewed by Ralph Abraham

Peter Demma was among the earliest pioneers of the Hip Culture of Santa Cruz in the 1960s. As documented in Volume 1 of this series, he arrived in Santa Cruz in 1963, from Palo Alto and the Kesey scene, and created the Hip Pocket Bookstore with Ron Bevirt. Melyssa, daughter of Peter and Karen Demma, was born into, and grew up with, Hip Santa Cruz. Here I talk with Melyssa about her childhood.

1. MILES STREET, 1965-69, ages 0-2 1/2

Ralph: So I thought I would start at the beginning, and go through your life, phase by phase. So, where were you born?
Melyssa: Santa Cruz, California, 1965.
Ralph: Tell me what your father and mother were doing at that time.
Melyssa: The Hip Pocket Bookstore opened in 1964 and closed in 1965. My father had been a couple of years into the Hip Pocket Bookstore when I was born. My most vivid early memory is smoking a cigarette. I was with Neal Cassady and the whole posse. I remember them looking really glamorous, so there's a photo of me with the cigarette.

I found a cigarette, I've got a kitten in my hand, and I remember this kitten too, because it was my first love, right? A kitten and a big stogie, it's a cigarette, not a cigar. We keep looking at it with like a loop to see if it's a joint, but I believe it's a rolled cigarette. Nobody else smoked cigarettes in my family or remembered anybody except for Neal Cassady, so it was obviously Neal's cigarette. I was so fascinated, and I do kind of remember him being somewhat of a buddy to me too. I was only 2-1/2. I can remember having my kitten and having a cigarette in my hand. The picture shows me taking a puff off it.

Ralph: Where were you living when you were 2-1/2?

Melyssa: This would have been on Miles Street over off of Mission Street.

Ralph: So tell me about your mother at that time.

Melyssa: So my mom — well, I was her second child and I believe that my dad was starting to really get into the social scene; just from reflections of what people say and memories of my own, my mom wasn't real fond of the whole posse and the social scene. She liked a little bit of it, daytime music, you know, for the bookstore I believe, and then when that whole scene went down, I think she pretty much stuck with it. I don't really remember anything having to do with the bookstore. I do remember living on Miles Street, though, and I do remember a lot of pretty good memories from there.

Ralph: So your mother was a full-time mom?

Melyssa: She was. And she was more about my dad being a bookstore owner, and I think that was the whole kind of, as you would say, a storefront. And she liked that part. That's my take, and that's what my family would say to me.

Ralph: After that you were still living on Miles Street?

Melyssa: Yes. My mom and aunt were there. I vaguely remember parties. I remember the street. I remember riding my little trike. And the dog we had. I remember getting bit on the lip by another dog who was protecting its babies. And my sister trying to climb out the top window, which was kind of strange.

2. THE BARN, 1966-69, ages 3-4

Melyssa: The Barn was kind of my beginning of my biggest memories. I remember a lot of live music. I remember

2 1/2 Lil Lyssie obsessed with kitten and Neal Cassady classic rolled cigarette. 1967, Miles Street.

sleeping to a lot of live music. By this point, the Barn definitely was a real scene and my mom really wanted out of the whole social scene with my dad. She kept threatening to not want to be a part of that, but she just wanted to be a little bit more of a normal family, the American way, kind of like living up to her dad. Her dad was more of a hard-nosed Italian and she was the firstborn, and she had to set or be a good example.

So '68 was the Barn, and I believe that right around that time was when my mom left. She started going for the Hell's Angels instead. She took her own life in '72.

Ralph: So when the Barn started up, Peter started going there and you met Joe Lysowski and Leon Tabory.

Melyssa: Papa Joe didn't really come into the scene until the Barn. Leon and I were always close. We've always been really close. And this is another whole — the Barn is like a huge thing, and I remember being in the Barn. I remember a lot of live music, all the time. That's the deepest part of my memory, which, sometimes it's tough for me now because I can't stand it if I don't have my comfort music around me now. And I remember a lot of live bands, definitely.

Ralph: I think you or maybe Ramah Tabory told me of an experience at the Barn when you were in a bathtub together. Do you remember that?

Melyssa: Yeah, I do.

Ralph: Were you living there?

Melyssa: No, we weren't living there. We were there a lot, though. But probably just from being out playing and whatever, out in the dirt out around us, it was like, and we've got a few photos of it. It's kind of out in the hills, kind of dirty. So I can imagine if I was a kid and I needed a bath — because there were a lot of women who would play with Ramah and Layla and myself — Layla was my older sister — it was like, it was all women, which is obviously why my mom was not happy. And the women just adored my dad. And so we always got a lot of attention from multiple women.

3. THE FLOWER FARM, 1969-71, ages 4-6

Melyssa: The next thing I remember is the Flower Farm. Ramah and I and Leon and my dad, were a big part of the Flower Farm. We lived in the commune there. I mean the Flower Farm was definitely right in the same time-frame as the Barn. So we must have been going back and forth. The Flower Farm was really cool.

Ralph: So tell me all about the Flower Farm. What was going on there, who lived there?

Melyssa: Here's what I remember. Bungalows and candles and lots of women. Lots of beat parties. Live music. If there wasn't live music and somebody wasn't playing, there was the Beatles all the time, there was a stereo with loudspeakers, and then there was somewhat of a more musical bonfire type party. And that was beautiful. I remember, I can smell it to this day. I can smell the beach and I can smell the flowers that were there. I visited it several times in my teens. It's at La Selva Beach, in between La Selva and Manresa. And there were mountains right there, it looked like only tractors could make it up, but I used to have a Volkswagen that would make it up one of the mountains and my friends and I would go up there and party or whatever. I was a teenager, and I remember wanting to go back to that, and getting that draft of that wonderful feeling and the smells.

Ralph: So who else lived there? Were there other people that are part of our story?

Melyssa: Leon Tabory did, and his kids. Cathy had already left him by then. It seems to me like the wives bailed out, like — No more! My mom said we need to go. I clearly remember her coming there, either to pick me up or people were picking me up, in between my dad and my mom. I think she was separated from him already. You know Lacy J. Dalton — her name was Jill Croston at the time? Jill and my mom, round about that time, these gals went more for the bikers. You get mad at your husband for being around a bunch of women but then go take off with the Hell's Angels.

4. BROOKDALE, 1971-74, ages 6-7-8

Melyssa: After the Flower Farm we moved to Brookdale. It wasn't a commune, but there were tiny little places, studio cabins that people lived in. I knew it as Brookdale Lodge but Brookdale Lodge is the hotel. We were across the street in a little wood cabin. That's where my dad met Renee. And then my mom started hanging out with fun biker dudes.

Okay, so my dad married Renee right after finding out that she was pregnant. That's when my mom took her life. The bikers had a drawer filled with pills, every kind that anybody wanted, and I guess she wanted them. I mean my mom actually committed suicide.

Ralph: So that was how she died?

Melyssa: Yeah. That time is the hardest time for me to just brush over because I think my mom was going to give my dad another chance, and then found out that Renee got pregnant, and then that was it.

So that's the hardest thing to go over in my life. But I'm 54. I just rationalized everything and then I tried to go into it and understand what happened, and now I know for a fact that she was going to try to get back together with him again.

So there is a time when I was with my dad and Renee, and Layla, my sister. She was the firstborn of my dad and my mom. But for whatever reason, Renee and Layla have always had a bond. They have a good relationship, and Layla stayed with Renee since my dad and Renee divorced. Renee always looked after Layla after that.

My dad ran for sheriff in 1973 on a marijuana platform. The posters all over town embarassed me.

5. CONTINENTAL STREET, 1974, age 8

Ralph: And after that?

Melyssa: Renee and my dad moved to Continental Street. Norman Gulliford lived across the street. It was a wonderful time. His mom was our landlady, and it was very idyllic, multi-cultural and multi-together. There were some very forthright classes where they sat down together in our living room with my dad and we could talk about other things of life from A to Z. I stayed with Renee and my dad until they divorced. My dad brought me up to be forgiving about the whole situation.

Chapter 14: Photo Gallery
by Andrew Bailey

Back in the Day (from the 1960s and 1970s)

Andrew Bailey by Ana De Abreu

Blue Bailey, 1972

Blue Hallock and Don Pierre, 1972

Don and Michael Open Sundays

Jeff and Wendy Love

Marcellus Barnes and T. Mike Walker

Max Hartstein

Ralph and Caroline Abraham

More Recent Portraits

Andrew Bailey

Al Lundell

Joe Lysowski

Leon Tabory

Nick Herbert

Patti DiLudovico

Peter Demma

Bruce Damer

David Oliver

Fred McPherson

Ralph Abraham

Dean Quarnstrom

T. Mike Walker

Jerry Kamstra

Chapter 15: One Night at The Barn
by Louie Bacigalupi

I was a "Teeny Bopper." This was back in 1967, going to Santa Cruz High School. Along with a group of other Teeny Bopper misfits and underachievers, commonly referred to as "Hippies," I hung out at Smoker's Corner right behind the school whenever I could. It was with this group that I began to frequent The Barn (in Scotts Valley).

I didn't know how strategic I was being when I bought my first car, but it was a 1955 Mercury-Monterey: a huge car. I could squeeze a whole lot of Teeny Boppers into that thing, so I was invited to lots of Santa Cruz parties that year. I also transported a large contingent of Teeny Boppers to the Barn regularly on Friday and Saturday nights. Little did I know what an influential part of my growth and evolution the Barn would become.

One night at The Barn was particularly memorable. The Smokers Corner bunch were all in a particular-frame-of-mind; exploring the boundaries between reality and what lies beyond. The band Bubble was playing. There was a liquid light projection show on the wall behind them. The strobe lights on the dance floor served to enhance the perception of exploring the outer boundaries of reality.

A little aside; who could imagine a bunch of high school kids talking about the nature of reality? But those conversations happened regularly. It was a time of spiritual renaissance and exploration. The adage youth is wasted on the young did not apply. A surprisingly high level of that youth from the Barn era has stayed with me until this day.

As we were enjoying the music, the lights, the ambiance (as well as our own particular-frame-of-mind), there came to be a disturbance that intruded itself into our world, bringing reality crashing back upon us. The Scotts Valley Police had raided The Barn. The smell of tear gas was unmistakable, even though I had never experienced it before I knew instinctively what it was. We were ordered to evacuate the building immediately. Things being as they were, we complied.

Outside of The Barn, the lines between reality and what lies beyond were blurred even further. There were police cars with flashing red lights blazing, and cops all around pointing flashlights into everyone's eyes: yelling and screaming. All I could do was to put one foot in front of the other, one step at a time until I miraculously found the way to my car.

Also having found their way to my car were my friends that I had ridden with me to the Barn that night. Additionally, there were several new friends I did not know I even had. It appeared that all my new friends needed a ride back to Santa Cruz as well.

There was one little problem that needed to be dealt with beforehand. Some of us were in possession of certain herbal remedies that we would just as soon keep as our little secret. Our use of these herbal remedies was strictly for medicinal purposes only, but we were concerned that the cops may not agree with that. To leave, we had to drive slowly past a bunch of cops who were intensely checking everyone out. It was likely they would want to search people as they drove away from the Barn. Of equal concern to us the thought of throwing away the herbal remedy and not having any to use for medicinal purposes.

So, we did what any teeny bopper would do in our place, we popped off one of my hubcaps and hid the various satchels of herbal remedy inside. As we popped the hubcap, we made coughing noises to cover the sound of the hubcap popping off and on. Thinking back on that years later, coughing sounds were probably not a good diversion to make at the time.

I stuffed 18 teeny boppers into my car that night. They sat three or four high on the seat, with a few laying along the rear windshield behind the back seat, and some stacked on the floor. I had to push hard on the car doors to get them shut as everyone inside exhaled. As I drove down Highway 17 from Scott's Valley to Santa Cruz that night, I had visions of the car doors flying open like a Jack-In-The-Box, with bodies bouncing along the freeway beside my car as I slowed down in horror.

I know not which set of gods it is that oversee teenyboppers in cars; but whomever they are, they were watching out for us that night. We made it back to Santa Cruz, car doors closed tight. As soon as we could, we retrieved our precious herbs from behind the hubcap, and each went their own way.

And we all lived happily ever after.

Beginning with my time at the Barn, I made life-long friendships with Leon Tabory and Peter Demma. Here is a picture my wife Suzanne took the last time I saw either of them. I would sure love to hang out with them again.

As we all would.

Chapter 16: Beard House, UCSC, 1967
by Douglas Col

I believe I have the honor of having helped to establish the original Beard House legacy. Mikel and I both started there in 1966, the first fall that the doors were opened (initially there wasn't even any carpets, just concrete). In fact, that's where I met Mikel.

However, it was the lower 4th floor that really gave Beard its original reputation. That pretty much started in the Fall and Winter of 1967, my second year in the same dorm room, when I made a connection through a friend in Stevenson and we were "importing" kilos of weed from the Hells Angels onto 4th floor Beard, where we broke up the kilos and put the weed on sheets of aluminum foil under beds, with Grow-Lux lights shining on the weed day and night (it converted more of the precursors to TCH, making the weed stronger). We had a thriving business selling "lids" (ounce baggies) of weed out of our floor.

We also had the distinction of having Herman Blake, then dorm preceptor (and Minister of Education for the Black Panther Party at the time) come up and excoriate us for smoking dope on the hall without bothering to close the door to the stairwell — he said that he came in the front entrance, and was hit by a wall of blue dope smoke.

One of our finer moments was when I managed to make a tool to break into the attic on our side of the dorm. We strung 700' of wire in the attic, creating a humongous antenna, and then ran a wire from that down into my closet, where we had a radio transmitter that we had cobbled together. Then we broke into the phone system wiring (wires going to each room, but no phone service yet) and were able to patch from my room, through the control panels (also broken into) on each hall, into John Kennedy's room on the second floor — since he had a good turntable and record connection. Thus was born KPOT, your "grass-roots" station from U.C. Santa Cruz.

We would play music and then get really stoned and go around campus at night with a wireless mic, doing "interviews" with other stoned (or not-stoned) students. It was great fun, though eventually we got pulled in by Crown College authorities. Turns out we were reaching people in Monterey (you've got to love a 700' antenna), and they had complained to the FCC. Crown College called me and another guy in, not because they could prove that we were doing anything (no one ever found the transmitter in my closet, or the antenna in the attic — which might still be there!) but because we were the only ones who they thought could be doing it (he and I were both physics students at the time).

The 4th floor Beard dynasty ended after my second year, when we threw a dorm party to end all dorm parties. We rolled a full kilo of weed into joints and divided the stash into shoe boxes that were placed in each hallway. There was a large buffet of food in one of the lounges, a belly dancer performing on one of the other lounge balconies, a rock band playing on a third balcony, and a jug band on the remaining balcony. There was also a trick of turning the light sensor on the top floor end of each external stairwell towards the light over the door at the top of that external stairwell. When you did that, the lights on all four floors — both on the external and the internal stairwell — flashed off and on on that side of the dorm. We did that for the two sides of the dorm, so that the lights were pulsing throughout the dorm. We had a San Francisco light show set up on the grass in front of the dorm, projecting a light show over the whole front of the dorm. The overall effect was psychedelic magic.

At roughly 2am Dean McHenry called Herman Blake and

made him shut us down, because the music was so loud that he couldn't sleep in the Chancellor's House down the hill from Beard. The next morning Herman, John Dizikes, and a couple of other faculty members were ordered to bust 4th floor Beard. They banged on our doors and demanded that we turn over our drugs to them. I dutifully went into my room, threw my stash out my window and gave them my seeds and stem collection. They confiscated all our weed, and later we all got suspended "for the "rest of the year," which was for 2 weeks at that point.

We had previously put together a little "side business" of breaking into the Cowell dining hall at night, and from there into the shared Cowell and Stevenson kitchen. We "opened" the walk-in refrigerated food storage room by simply taking the door off its hinges, and "requisitioned" essential materials like jelly rolls and a slab of ham for the munchies. Knowing how to break into things, we decided that our weed must be in the safe in Page Smith's office. We debated breaking in and reclaiming it, but decided at that point that discretion might be the better part of valor, so we demurred.

Many years later, at Page and Eloise Smith's memorial service at the Methodist church in Santa Cruz, I ran into Herman Blake. He looked at me and said "Doug Col, are you still alive?" I said "the last time I checked," but asked why he asked me that. He said "man, you were so out of control," to which I replied "Herman — I wasn't out of control. I was just out of YOUR control," and we laughed.

This is all to say that, at least at one point in history, Beard House — and particularly our 4th floor Beard — had a well-earned reputation (we'll talk later about the water balloon launcher that we made — we were able to launch water balloons from the 3rd floor lounge, over the dorm on the other side of the grassy area between the dorms, and hit

targets on the balcony of the dining hall.
  Keep the faith, y'all..

Index

A

Abraham, Ralph 5, 134, 149, 160
Alice, Mary 36
Aranda, Guillermo 63
Arconti, Ken 65
Arnetti, Jeff 65
Arnold, Jan 81
Arnold, John David 121, 129
Asawa, Ruth 56
Atchison, Rod 123

B

Bacigalupi, Louie 164
Bailey, Andrew 142, 150
Bailey, Blue 143
Baldwin, James 57
Baraka, Amiri 73
Bareis, Karl 83
Barnes, Marcellus 147
Barns, Marcellus 7
Bayez, Joan 7
Beagle, Peter 114
Bennett, Robert 114, 118, 120, 121, 125
Bessie, Dan 107
Bevirt, Ron 113, 114, 116, 118, 119, 120, 124, 130, 132, 133, 134
Blake, Herman 167, 168, 169
Bowers, Jack 55
Bowland, Kate 81
Bratton, Bruce 79
Brauer, Harry 113, 119, 124, 130
Braz-Valentine, Claire 63
Brezsny, Tom 25
Bristol, Roberta 11
Brooks, Laurie 63
Brown, Jerry 56
Brown, Ray 111
Brozman, Bob 87
Bryant, Martin 19

Bukowski, Charles 73
Burke, Bill 81
Burman-Hall, Linda 111

C

Caen, Herb 72
Carrillo, Eduardo 63
Cassady, Neal 43, 134, 136
Cervantes, Lorna Dee 74
Chappell, Walter 113, 116, 118, 129
Chavez, Cesar 29
Clarke, D. A. 19
Cochran, Jennifer 25
Cohen, Leonard 7
Col, Douglas 167
Coleman, Wanda 74
Cook, Mikel 167
Corso, Gregory 73
Coyote, Peter 56
Craft, Nikki 14, 16, 18, 19, 21
Crispo, Dick 58, 59, 60
Croston, Jill 64, 139

D

Dalton, Karen 7
Dalton, Lacy J. 64, 139
Damer, Bruce 157
Davidson, Ellen Gruys 62
De Abreu, Ana 142
Demma, Karen 134
Demma, Layla 137, 139, 140
Demma, Melyssa 134
Demma, Peter 113, 114, 116, 118, 119, 120, 121, 130, 132, 133, 134, 156, 166
de Palma, Frank 25
Deworker, John 19
DiLudovico, Patti 155
Di Prima, Diane 74
Dizikes, John 169
D., Michael 51, 52
Ducati, Tony 47, 49, 50
Dunbar, Tom 19
Dylan, Bob 7

E

Edwards, Betty 63
Ehrlich, Karen 93
Elliott, Ramblin' Jack 80
Ellison, Tom 25
Etcheverry, Elsa 84
Everson, William 74

F

Faith, Karlene 56
Felt, Joan 78, 79
Ferlinghetti, Lawrence 69, 72, 73
Flynt, Larry 15
Foreman, Judy and Frank 111
Fox, Michael 25
Furst, Tim 88, 90

G

Gallegos, Aaron 27
Garvison, John 114
Gere, Richard 72
Giese, Arthur 121
Ginsberg, Allen 73
Glass, Jonathan 27
Gossett Jr., Lou 7
Grodzins, Jim 83
Gruenich, Ray 18
Gulliford, Norman 140

H

Haavie, Robert 27
Hallock, Blue 144
Hann, Alfred 19
Harmon, Holly 8
Harper, Buddy 59
Harrison, Lou 31
Hartstein, Max 11, 74, 148
Havens, Richie 7, 10
Herbert, Nick 154
Herrera, Juan Felipe 57
Hill, Andrew 58

Hill, Kenny 64
Hinckle, Warren 71
Hogan, William 72
Holbert, Duncan 113, 114
Holmes, Mary 55
Hopper, Dennis 71
Hughes, Robert V. 124
Husband, Robert 123, 124, 128

J

Jackman, David 27
Jefferson, Thomas 126
Johnson, Al 30, 55
June, Roy E. 124, 130
June, Wanda 107

K

Kamstra, Jerry 68, 163
Kaufman, Bob 73
Kerouac, Jack 71, 72
Kerry, Theodora 20
Kesey, Ken 9, 31

L

Lang, Raven 84
Lee, Paul 55
Lenik, Paul 27
Lezin, Margaret 114
Lingemann, John 114
Lintz, Joan 25
Lira, Agustin 57
Little, Nita 83
Lloyd, Charles 73, 80, 81
Love, Jeff and Wendy 146
Lundell, Al 151
Lysowski, Joe 9, 137, 152

M

Marcus, Wilma 107
Marshall Krause 118
Martinez, Frank 19
Mathes, William 132

McCaslin, Don 11, 12, 111
McCleary, Katherine 84, 85
McHenry, Dean 168
McKee, Vern 56
McLean, Barrington 64
McLoughlin, Myra 114
McPhail, Ian 114
McPherson, Fred 159
Mello, Henry 58
Miller, Dan 113, 114
Miller, Henry 68, 74, 76
Miller, Jim 83
Modern, B. 18
Monkerud, Don 29
Moody, Graham 66
Moore, Elizabeth 113, 114

N

Nadeau, Scott and Joanna 85
Nahan, Kate 25
Neal, Fred 7
Nedelsky, Tom 83
Nelson, Jack 16
Newton, Huey 56
Nicosia, Gerald 72
Niven, Kathy 25
Noddy, Tom 86
Norgren, Jon 111
Notley, Chris 15

O

Oliver, David 158
Opalensces, Lolligo 26
Overton, Richard 123

P

Page, Aimee 27
Patterson, Ron & Phyllis 11
Pease, Richard 117, 118, 119, 120, 123, 124, 128
Peduto, Ralph 107
Phillips, Dan 106
Pierre, Don 144

Pini, Geno 117, 123
Pulley, Warden Reginald 58
Purifoy, Noah 56

Q

Quarnstrom, Dean 40, 161
Quentin, San 63

R

Ray, Chez 40, 41, 42, 45, 46, 53
Read, Ann 114
Reeves, Ron 113, 116, 120
Regardz, Beth 25, 26
Richards, Donald 24
Richards, M. C. 57
Richardson, Bruce 114, 121, 125
Richman, Jeff 21
Robbins, Tim 67
Rose, Annica 83, 84
Ross, Ralph 116
Ruiz, Roberta 64
Rydell, Frances 55
Rydell, Roy 31, 55

S

Sanders-Self, Nigel 63
Santana, Manny 29
Schultz, Jozseph 24
Schwarzenegger, Arnold 67
Scoppettone, James J. 118
Scott, David 77
Silver, Sam 73
Simonton, Ann J. 14
Slattum, Judy 107
Slick, Grace 82
Smith, Eloise Pickard 56, 57, 58
Smith, Page 55, 57
Smith, Page and Eloise 169
Stevens, Stanley D. 113
Steve Peterson 29
Stone, Victoria 16
Stuke, Noel 7

Sulski, Victoria 63

T

Tabory, Leon 121, 129, 137, 138, 153, 166
Tabory, Ramah 137, 138
Taves, Ted 31
Thierman, Eric 65
Thoreau, Henry 68
Thoth 87
Tichbourne, Roger 72
Trabing, Wally 113, 130
Troxel, Peter 81

V

Valenti, Dino 7, 10
Van Den Haag, Ernest 116
Vecchione, Patrice 108

W

Walker, T. Mike 5, 6, 7, 147, 162
Warren, Earl 60
Washkov, Irv 107
Wasserman, Ann 25
Waters, Alice 40
Weakland, Paul 19
Weeresekare, Raj 27
Welch, Gillian 87
Wenger, Daniel 75
Wiesinger, Steve 65
Williamson, Cris 20

Y

Yaryan, Daniel 68

Z

Zinnemann, Tim 72
Zoll, Julie 79, 81

www.ingramcontent.com/pod-product-compliance
Lightning Source LLC
Chambersburg PA
CBHW071713090426
42738CB00009B/1760